PENGUIN BOOKS

WHAT TYPE AM I?

Renee Baron is a writer, therapist, and public speaker. She is the coauthor of the best-selling books *Are You My Type, Am I Yours?* (Harper, 1995), *The Enneagram Made Easy* (Harper, 1994), and *The Four Temperaments* (St. Martins, 2004). She lives in Berkeley, California. Visit www.reneebaron.com.

PENGUIN BOOKS
Published by the Penguin Group
Penguin Group (USA) Inc., 375 Hudson Street, New York, New York 10014, U.S.A.
Penguin Books Ltd, 80 Strand, London WC2R 0RL, England
Penguin Books Australia Ltd, 250 Camberwell Road, Camberwell, Victoria 3124, Australia
Penguin Books Canada Ltd, 10 Alcorn Avenue, Toronto, Ontario, Canada M4V 3B2
Penguin Books India (P) Ltd, 11 Community Centre, Panchsheel Park, New Delhi – 110 017, India
Penguin Books (N.Z.) Ltd, Cnr Rosedale and Airborne Roads, Albany, Auckland, New Zealand
Penguin Books (South Africa) (Pty) Ltd, 24 Sturdee Avenue,
Rosebank, Johannesburg 2196, South Africa

Penguin Books Ltd, Registered Offices: 80 Strand, London WC2R 0RL, England

First published in Penguin Books 1998

20 19 18 17 16

Copyright © Renee Baron, 1998
All rights reserved

The Myers-Briggs Type Indicator® and MBTI are registered trademarks of Consulting Psychologists Press, Inc.

The inventory used in this book was written by the author based on her research of temperament and type in counseling and teaching. It is not a validated psychological assessment. If you wish to take the official Myers-Briggs Type Indicator (MBTI), refer to the resources in the back of this book.

Grateful acknowledgment is made for permission to use "Enneagram Types" from *The Enneagram Made Easy: Discover the Nine Types of People* by Renee Baron and Elizabeth Wagele. By permission of HarperCollins Publishers.

Illustrations by Miriam Fabbri

LIBRARY OF CONGRESS CATALOGING-IN-PUBLICATION DATA
Baron, Renee.
        What type am I?: discover who you really are/Renee Baron.
              p.   cm.
        ISBN 0 14 02.6941 X (pbk.)
        1. Typology (Psychology)   2. Temperament.   3. Myers-Briggs Type
        Indicator.   I. Title.
        BF698.3.B37   1998
        155.2′64—dc21   97-52023

Printed in the United States of America
Set in ITC Century Light
Designed by Kathryn Parise

What Type Am I?

Discover Who You Really Are

Illustrated by Miriam Fabbri

Renee Baron

PENGUIN BOOKS

He who knows others is learned;
He who knows himself is wise.
—LAO-TZU

In gratitude to my children Jodi, Tami "Luna," and Dan,
and to my friends who nurture, support, and encourage
my spiritual and emotional growth.

And to Sadie,
whose wisdom and clarity amaze and delight me.

Acknowledgments and Appreciations

I wish to express my deep appreciation to the following people. Without their efforts, this book would not have come to fruition.

To Tami "Luna" Baron, my daughter, friend, and editor for her clarity, insightfulness, and humor. Her suggestions have benefited each chapter of this book. I am grateful that she has taken interest in my work throughout the years.

To Miriam Fabbri for expressing my words and humor so creatively with her illustrations. It was a delight working together.

To Amanita Rosenbush for her enthusiasm in this project. Her clear mind and professional expertise were of great help.

To Richard Hendrickson of Career Works for his invaluable additions in the last few months of writing. His knowledge of type added a great deal to this project. I am especially grateful that my Higher Power brought him to me when I needed help with the final phase.

To my private clients and the thousands of workshop participants over the years who have helped make the types come to life.

To David Keirsey and Marilyn Bates, the authors of *Please Understand Me*, the book that started me on my journey of personality type. And to all the other authors whose books added to my knowledge.

To Dr. Linda Berens of the Temperament Research Institute for reading over the manuscript and offering feedback. Her suggestions were especially valuable in correcting some of my temperament biases.

To Beth Kuper for her editing and fine tuning. To Susan Urquhart-Brown for her editing, feedback, and promptness. To my dear friend Ellen Odza for helping me tie all the loose ends together. To Caryn Gottfried and Joan O'Connor for reading the entire manuscript, and to Eloise Mondfrans, Gary Pickler, Rich Byrne, and Naomi Friedman for reading individual chapters. To Rick Foster and Karen Keefer for phone interviews.

To Joyce Beckett for her helpful suggestions along the way and for adding to my knowledge of type in the beginning years of my studies.

To Susan Page for her counsel and encouragement throughout the years.

To Shelly Roth, my agent, for her support and professionalism.

To Jane von Mehren at Viking Penguin for her enthusiasm in the project and her excellent suggestions that gave the book more substance.

To Janet Hastings for listening each week to my ramblings, musings, anxieties, and joys.

My special thanks to Landry Wildwind for helping me to see the Truth and encouraging me to continue seeking my passion.

Contents

PART II
Temperaments and Types

Introduction

While I was growing up, every member of my family seemed so different from me. It felt as if I had been dropped into the wrong household. Wanting desperately to fit in, I tried very hard to please everyone and became pretty successful at it. Eventually I learned how to get my "strokes," gain acceptance, and evoke approval. Unfortunately, I had to pay a high price for this. My "natural self" remained hidden, not just to the world, but to myself as well. As a consequence, I grew up without developing many of my innate talents and gifts. Since I had put so much effort into being who my family wanted me to be, I lost any clear sense of who *I* really was.

As a result I was keenly aware of the qualities and abilities I didn't have. I was always comparing myself to others and putting myself down in subtle, and not so subtle, ways. When people would acknowledge my natural strengths and abilities by saying, "You have so many creative ideas," or, "You are very perceptive," I'd shrug it off because, like my parents, I didn't see these things as anything special.

After many years of therapy and an advanced degree in psychology, I discovered a book called *Please Understand Me* by David Keirsey and Marilyn Bates. It was about the Myers-Briggs system of personality typing as seen through the lens of Keirsey's temperament theory. Once I identified my own temperament and type, I was amazed because I recognized that it was so truly who I am. It gave me a strong sense of relief to finally identify my real Self. And then finding out that there were other people like me made me realize that I wasn't such a misfit after all.

The understanding and insight I gained was so uplifting to my self-esteem and sense of self-worth that I wanted to share it with others. And so, for the next eighteen years, I taught workshops in "self-acceptance," "career choices," and "positive parenting" through the use of personality temperaments and types.

One of my life goals has been to help parents accept, support, and encourage their children's natural temperament and personality type, rather than changing them so that they fit the parents' own picture of what their child should be. As a therapist I have witnessed a great deal of psychological and emotional damage to both young children and adult children because their parents had manipulated them in the name of "I only want what is best for you." The information in this book makes it clear that what is best for the child is to grow up and be what he or she was born to be, not just to fit in with its parents' image. Another of my goals is to help people learn to understand and accept themselves and to find meaningful careers based on their inherent talents, strengths, and abilities.

The study of personality temperaments and types was such a powerful tool for me that I knew it was important to teach it in the same way I had been introduced to it: the combination of temperament and type. The Jungian perspective on personality types explained my differences to me in a positive light. I read about what I fundamentally was, not what I should have been and wasn't. I discovered my true qualities and strengths, which I had previously rendered either invisible or valueless. What Jung basically said was "Don't try to be what you're not. Rejoice in your strengths." David Keirsey's perspective on temperaments, on the other hand, enabled me to understand the motivation behind the four groupings of the sixteen personality types. It explained my own core motivation, and showed me how different people really are from each other. What people really live for and what they seek out of life varies widely. This knowledge validated my lifelong need to live for my own authentic truth, for what gave my life meaning, not what had given my parents' life meaning. When I was introduced to the Myers-Briggs teaching, I experienced what is sometimes called the "Aha!"—that moment when you actually recognize yourself. It answered questions I had had all my life, and it helped me to see what my limitations were without being critical of them.

The more one delves into the Myers-Briggs system, the more complex it can get, and even the beginning level sometimes seems bewildering. While conducting research for this book, I interviewed hundreds of people who had taken the Myers-Briggs Type Indicator ® (MBTI). When I asked people what their type was, the response I got most often was "What are those letters again?" Very few people had actually made use of, or understood, the Myers-Briggs system and what it had to offer.

And so I will introduce you to the MBTI in the same way that it was taught to me, through the lens of Keirsey's temperament theory. This approach makes the sixteen types easier to understand. I have tried to keep the information as simple, yet informative, as possible. Part of my intention is also to present the information at a level that is understandable to teenagers so they can benefit as well. Once I learned personality theory, I wished I had been introduced to it at that stage of life; it would have given me tools for achieving the self-acceptance I so wanted and needed.

I hope that learning about personality type is as rich and rewarding for you as it has been for me, that it helps you to appreciate your innate strengths and abilities, and it enables you to live your life more in alignment with your true Self. It is also my wish that it helps you to understand, accept, and appreciate others.

What Type Am I?

Chapter 1

An Overview of the
Myers-Briggs System

Why do we feel that we have so much in common with some people, while others seem to be from a different planet? There has always been a basic human desire to understand why we are the way we are, and why others are the way they are. Each one of us is a unique individual, yet throughout history people have come up with systems to classify and categorize us into groups. The long tradition of classifying and labeling plants and animals has shown us that there are many benefits in classification—it is easier to understand and define a living thing's needs if we know what "type" it is.

As human beings, we can benefit from "typing" for the same reasons. The Myers-Briggs Type Indicator (MBTI), a system for understanding personality types, has a number of constructive and positive benefits. When we see that a person's usual style of behavior is part of a natural pattern, and not something that is "wrong," it makes it easier to view our own behavior and that of others with less judgment. Recognizing that the style, values, and tendencies are inherent to who they are makes it less confusing and, consequently, less irritating for us when that style happens to differ from our own. That gives us the ability to develop a more objective view of other people's ways so that we do not take remarks or actions personally when they are, in fact, not directed at us, but simply part of their makeup.

When we understand and nurture ourselves for who we are, we have a chance to excel in ways that suit our natural abilities. We also have a more solid foundation from which to interact with others who have a different style.

Self-understanding and acknowledgment can lead us to more appropriate and rewarding career choices.

Learning about personality types can also help us make more conscious choices in relationships. It will enable us to see why, although we are initially drawn to a certain type of person, we are ready to tear our hair out about their habits and "shortcomings" a few months later. Sometimes the very same quali-

ties that attracted us to someone in the first place are the ones that we find ourselves trying to change later on.

Once we understand other personality types, we can have more compassion and support for who they are and encourage the characteristics and behaviors that are important to them. We can support and nurture the qualities that they value, not just the ones we value. When we allow others to be who they are, offering acceptance instead of judgment, we are reflecting back to that person the gift of their true Self. Learning about personality types affords us the opportunity to create more harmony and understanding in our lives and in the lives of those around us.

OVERVIEW

In this book, there are three words you will be hearing over and over: preference, type, and temperament. As we go along, the differences and nuances will be further defined, but for now, here is a brief look at the overall system to see what these terms mean and how they interrelate:

Preferences

The system that Myers-Briggs came up with to understand personality differences basically describes different patterns of behavior, all of which affect and determine how we function in the world. The system is based on the idea that people are born with preferences. The word *preference* simply refers to the ways in which we naturally "prefer" to do certain things.

Myers-Briggs list four pairs of opposite preferences. Within each pair, we favor one side over the other, and we tend to use that one most of the time because it comes more easily to us.

The four pairs of opposite preferences are:

Extraverting (E) and Introverting (I)

This pair refers to where we prefer to focus our attention and what energizes us. *(Note: Jung and MBTI literature consistently spells the word "Extravert" with an "a" which is the way it will appear in this book.)*

Sensing (S) and iNtuiting (N)

This pair refers to how we prefer to take in information.
(Note: The letter N is used for iNtuiting because I is used for Introverting.)

Thinking (T) and Feeling (F)

This pair refers to how we evaluate information and make decisions.

Judging (J) and Perceiving (P)

This pair refers to our lifestyle orientation.

Type

Within each pair of opposite preferences a person leans toward one or the other. Taking one preference from every pair will form the four-letter code that represents each person's type. For example, if a person prefers Extraverting, Sensing, Thinking, and Judging their type is ESTJ. All together there are sixteen different types. As with many other things in life, the combination of individual preferences is greater than the sum of its parts. They interact in different ways and in varying degrees to make each person unique.

Temperament

Temperament theory suggests that we all have a certain fundamental desire that propels us, that is what we live for. Some people, for example, live for spontaneity and freedom and some for duty, some live for control and understanding of the world while others live for self-realization and understanding of the self. A person's temperament largely determines how his or her behavior will gather into "activity patterns." This means that within all the activities people engage in throughout their lives, you can see a continuous thread of motivation.

What has been recognized throughout the centuries is that there are four basic categories of temperament that people tend to fall into; they are based on the core themes in their lives. These categories have been referred to by many names, but in this book, they are:

Duty Seekers   Knowledge Seekers
Action Seekers   Ideal Seekers

Understanding the four temperaments makes the sixteen personality types easier to grasp as each temperament is the root of four different personality types.

A Brief History

Type and *temperament* actually represent two separate systems of classifying personalities, which later converged. The type system comes from the work of Jung, and of Myers and Briggs. And the second system, temperament, was compiled by David Keirsey.

The personality type theory model on which the MBTI is based was developed by the Swiss psychoanalyst Carl Jung. His assertion was that the reason we may be classified or "typed" by our particular preferences is that they are characteristic of our basic nature, meaning they are a fundamental part of who we are. An American woman named Katherine Briggs had been developing a personality theory of her own when she read Jung's system. Because it so clarified her thinking on the subject, she adopted it. In the 1940s she and her daughter, Isabel Myers, developed a questionnaire about preferences that is now known as the Myers-Briggs Type Indicator (MBTI). It was designed to help people determine their personality types. It divided them into sixteen types based on their preferences. Today, the MBTI is the most widely used psychological instrument in the world. It has been translated into fourteen languages, and more than ten million copies of the English version have been sold in the last five years.

Temperament theory, in contrast, has actually been around in various forms for about twenty-five centuries, dating back to Hippocrates. He observed four basic configurations of behavior in people and called them temperaments. His labels were: choleric, phlegmatic, melancholic, and sanguine. In the recent past, others have developed their own spin on the idea of temperaments. Among them were Four world views (Adickes), Four different makes (Adler), Four human values (Spranger), and so on.

In 1978, temperament theory was revived by an American clinical psychologist named David Keirsey. Keirsey reviewed the temperament ideas from the past, and arrived at his own configuration. When he came upon the Myers-Briggs descriptions of the sixteen types, he saw within them the temperament patterns that he had been writing about. In his book *Please Understand Me*, he outlines his four temperaments, correlating them with the sixteen types of the Myers-Briggs system.

Even though type and temperament theory evolved separately, they have been found to overlap and complement each other in ways that make studying them together very beneficial. Both the Jung/Myers-Briggs type theory and the Keirsey temperament theory offer an approach to personality that explains things in a helpful, practical, and often profound way.

Some Suggestions for Getting the Most Out of This Book

Take your time reading each of the preference chapters in Part I. Make it a process of self-observation and self-discovery. Each preference has its own richness and can answer long-held questions about yourself and others. The preferences provide the tools for understanding the entire Myers-Briggs system.

There is no right way to read this book. Different personality types are going to approach it with their own perspective. Some might start from the beginning and read it all the way through; some will estimate their type and go right to that description; some will want to look for their partner's, friend's, or children's type. Approach the material in whatever style feels most natural to you.

Part I

The Preferences

Chapter 2

An Introduction to Preferences

A preference is an inborn tendency to be, act, or think in a certain way. While we do change and grow, and may seem to be different at various times in our lives, our basic personality style remains the same. For example, Thinkers never becomes Feelers; they may, however, develop their Feeling side and use it more often.

As you read through the Inventories that follow, you may identify somewhat with both preferences in a pair, but there will be one that you rely upon more comfortably and gravitate toward naturally. Your preference is the one that comes most easily and automatically; its opposite is the one that is less familiar and that you tend to struggle with.

To explain it another way, stop now and write your name the way you always do. Now write it a second time using the opposite hand. While you are doing that, pay attention to what the experience is like. Writing with the hand you use every day is effortless, and you don't even think about it. It is something you can do with your eyes closed. When you use your other hand, it probably feels awkward, it takes more time, and you have to concentrate more. Put simply, you do things more comfortably and efficiently with the hand you prefer, the one you use most naturally and instinctively.

No preference is better or worse than its opposite, just as no personality style is smarter, more moral, or makes a better husband, wife, child, worker, or friend. They are simply different. Each has natural strengths and each has potential weakenesses.

In the hundreds of activities we engage in each day, we can, and often do, use both preferences. We couldn't function well if we didn't. But we do not use them with equal frequency, ease, or success. And although we can use both, we do not use both at once. When one preference comes into the foreground, the other one recedes. For example, if we are engaging in an activity where we have to make logical, objective, thinking decisions, we pay little attention to the subjective, personal, feeling side of ourselves. Using the appropriate preference in the appropriate situation is a natural and practical way to function in the world.

Different preferences are also experienced in varying degrees. Within certain pairs, for instance Sensing and iNtuiting, we may have strong tendencies toward one side, while with another pair, for instance Judging and Perceiving, we may be more dexterous with either preference. Having a strong preference, however, does not mean that our ability or competence is better. Preferences and abilities are not the same thing. In fact, it can be desirable to practice using the opposite of our preferred style because the more we use any preference, intentionally or unintentionally, the more available it is to us when we need it.

People often find that at certain times in their lives, particular preferences will be stronger or weaker. As people mature, for example, they develop more familiarity with their nonpreferences. Even so, the nonpreference never takes the place of the favored preference.

The System

The MBTI system identifies four basic dimensions of human personality, each dealing with an important aspect of life. This is the reason personality typing gives us such accurate insights into our own and into other people's behavior. The preferences are listed in four pairs of opposites:

The two ENERGIZING preferences: EXTRAVERTING (E) and INTROVERTING (I)

- Those who prefer Extraverting get their energy from the outer world of people, activities, and things.
- Those who prefer Introverting get their energy from their inner world of ideas, impressions, and thoughts.

The two INFORMATION GATHERING preferences: SENSING (S) and INTUITING (N)

- Those who prefer Sensing pay attention to information taken in directly through their five senses and focus on *what is* or *what was.*

- Those who prefer iNtuiting pay attention to their sixth sense, to hunches and insights, and they focus on *what might be*.

The two DECIDING preferences: THINKING (T) and FEELING (F)

- Those who prefer Thinking make decisions in a logical and objective way.
- Those who prefer Feeling make decisions in a personal, values-oriented way.

The two LIFESTYLE ORIENTATION preferences: JUDGING (J) and PERCEIVING (P)

- Those who prefer Judging tend to live in an organized, planned way.
- Those who prefer Perceiving tend to live in a spontaneous, flexible way.

Finding Your Preferences

For every set of preferences there is a list of ten statements called an Inventory. Read each statement carefully, and then use the following numbers to indicate your response.

0—not like me at all
1—somewhat like me
2—exactly like me

To get a score that is a reflection of your true preference, put down your first response. Be aware of projecting the characteristics you want to have as opposed to the ones you actually have. Answer as your "at home self" rather than your "at work self," where you may have to use preferences that are not true to your type. In each set, the list of statements with the highest score is probably your preference for that pair.

Following the Inventory is a list of paired words. Read them and see which column of words best describes you. See if this matches your Inventory results. Then proceed to read the rest of the information in each chapter. At the end of each chapter there is a place to estimate which preference you believe you are.

Chapter 3

Extraverting (E) vs Introverting (I)

The Energizing Preferences:
Where We Get Our Energy

THE INVENTORY

Read each statement and use the following numbers to indicate your responses.

0—not like me at all
1—somewhat like me
2—exactly like me

Extraverting (E)

_____ 1. I get energized by socializing and talking with people.

_____ 2. I am relatively easy to get to know and most people find me friendly, outgoing, and enthusiastic.

_____ 3. I am comfortable being with and meeting new people.

_____ 4. I enjoy being the center of attention.

_____ 5. I'm quite talkative and often prefer verbal over written communication.

_____ 6. I can find something to talk about with almost anyone.

_____ 7. I have many friends and acquaintances.

_____ 8. I feel lonely and restless if I spend long periods of time alone.

_____ 9. I have to monitor myself to make sure I allow others a chance to speak.

_____ 10. I develop my ideas and reach conclusions by talking. I tend to think out loud.

_____ TOTAL

Introverting (I)

_____ 1. I feel awkward at social events where I don't know many people, but I enjoy talking one-on-one with someone I feel connected to.

_____ 2. I like to spend a lot of time alone.

_____ 3. I tend to have a few close friends on whom I focus most of my attention, rather than a lot of acquaintances.

_____ 4. Instead of approaching others, I wait for them to approach me.

_____ 5. People often perceive me as shy or aloof.

_____ 6. I take time to consider what I am going to say before I speak.

_____ 7. I feel drained if I spend a lot of time with people. Even talking on the phone for too long can be exhausting.

_____ 8. I prefer to work by myself on projects and tasks.

_____ 9. I am very selective and particular about who I will begin friendships with.

_____ 10. I avoid being the center of attention.

_____   TOTAL

The following list of paired words summarizes the key characteristics of Extraverts and Introverts. Which list desribes you best?

Extraverts	Introverts
seek interaction	like to be alone
enjoy groups	enjoy one-on-one
act or speak first, then think	think first, then speak or act
expend energy	conserve energy
focus outwardly	focus inwardly
talkative	quiet
like variety and action	like to focus on one thing at a time
outgoing	reserved
think out loud	think to themselves
enjoy discussing	enjoy reflecting

In the context of this system, Extraversion does not mean talkative, and Introversion does not mean shy. The two words refer to whether a person gets energized in the outer world or their inner world.

Extraverts are outgoing, enthusiastic, often fast-paced, and enjoy a lot of interaction.

To understand the world, they need to experience it. Their tendency is to act, discuss, or process verbally, and then act some more. They often think out loud and find it fairly easy to talk to anyone. They get rejuvenated by being with people and feel drained when they're alone. Extraverts prefer to focus their attention on the outer world and get energized by interacting with people, things, and activities in the external world.

Introverts are often reserved and private. They need more time to themselves and tend to conserve their energy. They want to understand the world before they experience it and often think and reflect before acting or speaking. Interacting too much with others can drain their energy. To rejuvenate, they need to be by themselves or in silence. Introverts prefer to focus their attention inward and get energized by their internal world of ideas, impressions, and thoughts.

When an Introvert and an Extravert are in a relationship, the differences in their preferences can be a source of tension and conflict. They sometimes have a difficult time understanding each other even if their other three preferences (Sensing/iNtuiting, Thinking/Feeling, Judging/Perceiving) are the same. To an Extravert, Introverts can seem withholding, antisocial, boring, and uninterested. Their quiet ways can drive an Extravert crazy! To an Introvert, Extraverts can seem pushy, intrusive, hyper, and too talkative. Their running commentary on life can drive an Introvert crazy!

As with all the personality preferences, people need to make allowances for differences instead of assuming others' behavior is wrong because it doesn't match their own. Introverts often feel pressured to conform to extraverted standards of behavior since their quiet ways and desire for time alone is interpreted as antisocial behavior. Understanding the Introvert's need for quiet and the Extravert's need for sociability is important. Without this acceptance it is difficult to maintain a noncritical attitude in a relationship.

How to get along with Extraverts

The only way to entertain some folks is to listen to them.
—AUTHOR

- Appreciate their ability to initiate activities and conversations.
- Give them plenty of acknowledgment and attention.
- Listen to them talk so they can sort things out and clarify their ideas.
- Go out and do things with them. Interact in the world with them.
- Understand their need to be with other friends besides you.

AN EXTRAVERT'S PARTY WITH HER 50 CLOSEST FRIENDS.

How to get along with Introverts

That man's silence is wonderful to listen to.
—THOMAS HARDY

- Respect their need for time alone.
- Give them time to think and sort things out on their own.
- Respect their need to have certain matters kept private.
- Try to edit your thoughts before speaking.
- Spend time with them in silence, doing things together "alone."
- Do not pressure them to socialize or interact with a lot of people.

Suggestions for Extraverts

SAM WAS SO EXCITED ABOUT WHAT HE WAS SAYING THAT HE DIDN'T NOTICE NO ONE ELSE WAS.

- Experiment with processing your thoughts and feelings in writing or meditation instead of verbally.
- Beware of excessive talking. Remember to take notice of people's interest or lack of interest in what you are saying.
- Make sure you have plenty of time with others. Don't leave long blocks of time to be alone if you are highly Extraverted.
- Don't rely on an Introverted mate or friend for all of your social needs.
- Stimulate yourself with the outer world when you need to get charged up. If there's no one to hang out with, go to a busy café or an event.
- Take time to think things through and to explore issues in more depth before taking action.
- To discover your inner self, engage in activities you enjoy that do not involve being with other people (walks in nature, reading, crafts, painting, meditation, etc.).

What a lovely surprise to discover how un-lonely being alone can be.
—ELLEN BURSTYN

Suggestions for Introverts

- Don't feel guilty for needing privacy or solitude.
- Learn to compromise with your family and friends and negotiate time together as well as time apart.
- Instead of always waiting for your partner, family,

and friends to ask you to join them for activities, take the initiative some of the time and ask them.

- Challenge yourself to speak up in groups. Remind yourself that your opinions and thoughts are important and valuable.
- Rather than processing things internally and just sharing your final conclusions, try talking about things as they come up.
- If you go to a large event or a party, try to have at least one close friend there for support and to check in with. Take your own car so you know you can leave whenever you're ready.
- Be generous and expressive with compliments and praise (especially with Extraverts).

Now that you've read about Extraversion and Introversion you probably have a good idea of what your preference is. (If not, guess for now.)

I think my preference is:

(E) _____   (I) _____

Turn to page 40 and write E or I in the first box. This is the first letter of your four-letter type. If your score was very close, you can write both E and I for now. Use a pencil since you may want to change your type estimate as you learn more.

Chapter 4

Sensing (S) vs INtuiting (N)

The Information Gathering Preferences:
How We Take in Information

THE INVENTORY

Read each statement and use the following numbers to indicate your responses.

0—not like me at all
1—somewhat like me
2—exactly like me

Sensing (S)

_____ 1. I tend to be practical, realistic, and matter-of-fact.

_____ 2. I'm more interested in facts and figures than in theories.

_____ 3. I prefer tasks that have a practical application and produce tangible results.

_____ 4. I tend to speak, hear, and interpret things literally.

_____ 5. I'm a good observer. I notice my surroundings and often remember the details.

_____ 6. I like hands-on projects such as making model cars, assembling things, or doing needlework.

_____ 7. I like utilizing and developing the skills I already have.

_____ 8. I have a great capacity for enjoying the here and now and am often content to let things be.

_____ 9. I trust my personal experiences of what is real and certain.

_____ 10. I focus on what is at hand rather than speculating too far in the future.

_____ TOTAL

iNtuiting (N)

_____ 1. It can be hard for me to stay focused on the present because I often speculate about several ideas at once.

_____ 2. I tend to use metaphors and analogies when describing or explaining something.

_____ 3. I rely on hunches, inspiration, and imagination for a lot of my information.

_____ 4. I like to think about new possibilities and focus on what "might be."

_____ 5. I am oriented toward the future and like to do things in untried and innovative ways. I dislike routine and repetition.

_____ 6. I look for underlying patterns and "the big picture." I don't like getting caught up in specific details.

_____ 7. I watch for, and pay attention to, implications and inferences.

_____ 8. I "read between the lines" and imagine or speculate about what is not stated.

_____ 9. I pay little attention to what is going on in my immediate surroundings. I can be very unaware of the here and now.

_____ 10. I enjoy abstractions and theories and sometimes find the details of everyday life boring.

_____ TOTAL

The following pairs of words or phrases summarize the key characteristics of Sensing and iNtuiting preferences. Which describe you best?

Sensors	_INtuitives_
prefer facts, concrete information	prefer insights, abstract information
are more interested in what is actual	are more interested in what is possible
pay attention to specifics	focus on the big picture
are practical and realistic	are inspired and imaginative
focus on the present	focus on the future
value common sense	value innovation
are pragmatic	are speculative

| trust their past experience | trust their imagination and hunches |
| tend to want things as they are | tend to want to try something new |

Those who prefer Sensing tend to take in information mainly through their five senses: what they can see, hear, taste, touch, and smell in the "real" world. They pay attention to facts and the specific data that come to them through their sensory awareness. They focus more on what actually exists than on possibilities. "What is" is more useful than "what might be." Those who prefer Sensing tend to record the world as they see it, at face value, in the moment. They notice what is right in front of them and rely on what can be measured or documented. They value common sense and trust their past experience and the established ways of doing things. Sensors appreciate the concrete realities of a situation and work with what is given. They tend to describe things literally and expect others to do the same. They have little need to interpret underlying meanings or assumptions about things.

Those who prefer iNtuiting also take in information through their fives senses, but they pay more attention to their sixth sense—their hunches and insights. They read between the lines, looking for underlying meanings that go beyond what is in front of them. They are at home with abstract, intangible information. They perceive the relationship between things in an associative way and look for the patterns and interconnections between things. When they describe what they "see," they jump around wherever their intuition takes them, and prefer not to be literal or follow a sensible sequence. They prefer to notice what might be there or what it could become, instead of what is. iNtuitives are interested in possibilities and are open to change. They value inspiration more than common sense or the tried and true.

Sensors and iNtuitives see the world in fundamentally different ways and often fail to appreciate each other's perspective. Communication can be difficult between them because they see things so differently, and each believes that his or her information is more accurate, valid, and real.

How to get along with Sensors

- Appreciate how much they accomplish by being realistic, down-to-earth, and practical.
- When communicating with them, stick to the facts and issues at hand. Use real and concrete examples. Be explicit.
- Stress the practical application of your ideas if you want them to be accepted.

- When explaining how to do something, give step-by-step instructions.
- Engage with them in activities of the senses (sports, gardening, crafts, home projects, etc.).

WHAT ANNOYS SENSORS

WHAT ANNOYS INTUITIVES

How to get along with iNtuitives

- Appreciate them for their inventive minds, original ideas, and their ability to solve problems creatively.
- Don't inundate them with facts or burden them with unnecessary details.

- Listen to them when they ponder new concepts and possibilities and participate with them in fantasizing about new ideas.
- Trust their ability to gather information through their hunches. Don't always question them about why or how they "know."

Suggestions for Sensors

- Avoid arguing about specifics when having discussions or disagreements, especially when dealing with iNtuitives.
- Allow time to look beyond the obvious and to imagine new possibilities for

handling or changing a situation. Refrain from automatically ruling out ideas that seem impractical.
- Try listening to what may seem remote or fanciful. Play with your own imagination.
- Learn to acknowledge other ways of knowing, including hunches, dreams, and fantasies.
- To further develop your iNtuition, consider a class in creative writing or read books on philosophy, mysticism, and psychic phenomena. Have discussions about the meaning of life.

Suggestions for iNtuitives

- Be open to hearing feedback on the practical reality, feasibility, and possible pitfalls of your ideas and visions.
- Try not to always live in the future. Practice being in the here and now.
- Plan a project and make yourself write down what is involved step-by-step before beginning it.
- To further develop your Sensing skills, consider a cooking class, give and receive massages, try arts and crafts, exercise, hike, garden, or do home repair; try to keep your attention on your physical sensations and surroundings.

- Take time to notice how things look, listen, smell, feel, sound, and taste. Indulge your senses once in a while.

Now that you've read about Sensing and iNtuiting you probably have a good idea of what your preference is. If you're not sure, guess for now.

I think my preference is:

(S) _____   (N) _____

Turn to page 40 and write S or N in the second box for the second letter of your four-letter type. If your score was very close, you can write both S and N for now. Use a pencil so you can make changes later.

Chapter 5

Thinking (T) vs Feeling (F)

The Deciding Preferences: How We Evaluate Information and Make Decisions

The Inventory

Read each statement and use the following numbers to indicate your responses.

0—not like me at all
1—somewhat like me
2—exactly like me

Thinking (T)

_____ 1. I value my ability to think and make decisions logically and clearly.

_____ 2. I like to debate and defend my point of view. Sometimes, just to challenge my intellect, I argue both sides of an issue.

_____ 3. I have been accused of not paying attention to other people's needs and feelings.

_____ 4. People sometimes see me as impersonal and overly analytical.

_____ 5. I can be blunt and outspoken.

_____ 6. I tend to pay attention to others' thoughts more than to their feelings.

_____ 7. I don't like to put my emotions on display.

_____ 8. I usually make decisions based on the general principles of justice and logic more than on personal circumstances or concerns.

_____ 9. I consider it more important to be truthful than tactful.
_____ 10. I don't shy away from critiquing or correcting people.
_____ TOTAL

Feeling (F)

_____ 1. I value my ability to be empathetic and compassionate.
_____ 2. I like to talk about interpersonal relationships and emotions.
_____ 3. In my decision-making process, how others will be affected carries a lot of weight.
_____ 4. It is important to be tactful as well as truthful.
_____ 5. Being appreciated and approved of are very important to me.
_____ 6. I look for what is good in people and things.
_____ 7. People tend to seek me out for warmth and nurturing.
_____ 8. I have trouble speaking up about what I want or need.
_____ 9. When I disagree with people, it is difficult for me to tell them.
_____ 10. I take criticism very personally and I have been accused of being too sensitive.
_____ TOTAL

The following list of paired words summarizes the key characteristics of Thinking and Feeling preferences. Which describes you best?

Thinkers	*Feelers*
are firm-minded	are gentle-hearted
analyze the problem	sympathize with your problem
are objective, convinced by logic	are subjective, convinced by values
are direct	are tactful
value competence	value relationships
decide with their head	decide with their heart
value justice	value harmony
can be seen as insensitive	can be seen as overemotional
are good at critiquing	are good at appreciating
usually don't take things personally	usually take things personally

Those who have a preference for Thinking make decisions through a logical, analytical process and seek an objective standard of truth. When making decisions, they place more value on consistency and fairness than on how others will be affected. They examine and weigh the logical consequences of their choices and actions. They look for flaws and falacies, excelling at critiquing conclusions and pinpointing what is wrong with something. *Thinking* usually refers to using the intellect, but in this context it simply means that Thinkers make decisions more analytically and impersonally.

Feeling often suggests emotionality. Here, it does not mean that those who have a preference for Feeling are more emotional. It simply means that they make decisions more subjectively, according to their values or what is more important to them. They also place greater emphasis on how other people will be affected by their choices and actions. Those who prefer Feeling pay a lot of attention to all their relationships because these are high on their values list. Their truth is based on personal and social values. It is possible for them to decide whether something is acceptable or agreeable without needing logical reasons.

Remember that although Thinkers' feelings are not always visible, they do have them, and that even though Feelers may not always verbalize their logic, they are completely capable of logical thought. The two simply use different criteria for making decisions—logic versus values. When these two ways of decision-making are understood and appreciated, they can complement each other in a relationship instead of causing problems.

WHAT ANNOYS THINKERS

WHAT ANNOYS FEELERS

Some people find it difficult to determine whether they prefer Thinking or Feeling because their true preference may go against their conditioning, especially if it is along gender lines. Women are often socialized to behave like Feelers and men are often socialized to behave like Thinkers. Therefore, Thinking females and Feeling males are socially in the minority and probably have been made to feel unaccepted.

How to get along with Thinkers

- Appreciate their insightful analysis and their ability to remain calm and detached.
- Ask them for information or advice on something they know a lot about.
- Don't force them to talk about or display their emotions.
- Ask them what they think, rather than how they feel.
- Allow them to express their criticisms of situations and people without becoming reactive or defensive. Listen for the points you agree with and say so.
- Be willing to express your disagreements without worrying about it being unkind or starting an argument. You're entitled to your opinion. Thinkers may want to argue for fun but they'll respect you for having and holding your view.

How to get along with Feelers

The best way to compliment someone is frequently.
—ANONYMOUS

- Let them know you appreciate their warmth, understanding, and compassion.
- Acknowledge their ability to express their feelings and help people be at ease.
- Don't use sarcasm or tell them they're being illogical.
- Have personal conversations with them and focus on what you agree upon.
- Don't tell them they're too sensitive or too emotional.
- Listen to their concerns. Unless they specifically ask for advice, don't try to solve their problems. They often bring up a subject just because they want to talk things through.

Suggestions for Thinkers

- Consider what impact your feedback will have on the other person. Begin with the positive, and then try to present things in a way that will be easy to hear. For example, "The color is nice, but the shirt seems too big in the shoulders" instead of "That shirt looks terrible on you."

- Beware of giving too much of what you consider "constructive" criticism. You may think you're helping, or being accurate, but others may perceive that they are constantly being corrected.

- When relating with Feeling types, avoid taking an opposing stance just for the sake of debating the fine points. Arguing only puts them off and creates distance.

- Learn to be more generous with praise, encouragement, and appreciation. Express your warm feelings and get syrupy once in a while.

- Apologize once in a while. Allow yourself to lose an argument. Then congratulate yourself on both feats. Make "I'm sorry" and "You're right" part of your vocabulary.

- For developing your Feeling preference, try classes in psychology, go for counseling or group therapy, volunteer at a hospice.

- Learn to be a little more vulnerable in circumstances where it is appropriate.

- In order to assess your own and others' feelings, pay attention to their body language or to your own body sensations.

- Consider how other people will feel about various plans and outcomes before making your final decision.

Suggestions for Feelers

Learn to say "no." It will be of more use to you than to be able to read Latin.
—CHARLES HADDON SPURGEON

- Learn to ask for what you want. Avoid answering with "It doesn't matter" or "Whatever you want is fine with me."
- Speak up if you feel you are being treated unfairly or being taken advantage of. Learn to negotiate, set limits, and be direct.

- Avoid talking excessively about your feelings when with Thinkers.

- Try to evaluate your options objectively and to think things through before deciding.
- Find work in environments that are friendly, supportive, and cooperative.
- Learn to detach and not take criticism so personally. Practice observing your reactions calmly without getting caught up emotionally.
- Consider classes in statistics, science, economics, or logic to develop your Thinking preference. Learn to play chess or bridge.

Now that you've read about Thinking and Feeling you probably have a good idea of what your preference is. If not, guess for now.

I think my preference is:

(T) _____   (F) _____

Turn to page 40 and write T or F in the third box representing the third letter of your four-letter type. Remember, if your scores are very close, you can write both down and decide which is more accurate once you've learned more.

Chapter 6

Judging (J) vs Perceiving (P)

The Living Preferences:
What Lifestyle We Prefer

THE INVENTORY

Read each statement and use the following numbers to indicate your responses.

0—not like me at all
1—somewhat like me
2—exactly like me

Judging (J)

_____ 1. I dislike having things undecided.

_____ 2. I find it hard to relax or concentrate if my environment is disorganized or cluttered.

_____ 3. I make "to do" lists and feel satisfied when I check off a completed task.

_____ 4. I have my particular ways of doing things. I don't like it when others try to change my schedule, especially at the last minute.

_____ 5. I like to have a place for everything and have everything in its place.

_____ 6. Before beginning a task or project, I like to review what I'll need and make sure everything's on hand.

_____ 7. It's important to me to be on time, and I can't understand when this isn't a priority to others.

_____ 8. I like to know what the schedules and time frames are. If there's no plan, I feel uneasy.

_____ 9. I don't like to leave a task undone, and I much prefer to finish one project before starting another.

_____ 10. I need to finish my work before I can relax and have fun.

_____ TOTAL

Perceiving (P)

_____ 1. I am relatively easygoing, adaptable, and flexible. When there are last-minute changes, I just adapt to them.

_____ 2. It's not that I lack focus, I just have my own way of going back and forth from one project to another.

_____ 3. I like to start new projects; I'll usually start the next one before finishing the one I'm on.

_____ 4. Being on schedule is not the most important thing in my life. Deadlines give me a general idea of when something's due.

_____ 5. I don't usually make "to do" lists, but if I do, going back to check things off is not important. Writing things down is reminder enough.

_____ 6. I often wait until a deadline is near before focusing on completing a task.

_____ 7. My way of organizing my room or work space can appear chaotic to others.

_____ 8. I don't need to complete all my tasks or work before I can relax or play.

_____ 9. My tendency is to postpone making decisions, often gathering more information, until it is absolutely necessary to decide.

_____ 10. I welcome opportunities for spontaneity. I enjoy the unexpected.

_____ TOTAL

The following list of paired words summarizes the key characteristics of Judging and Perceiving preferences. Which describe you best?

Judging	_Perceiving_
seek closure	seek openness
value structure	value the flow
plan ahead	adapt as they go
like order	like flexibility
work now/play later	play now/work later

like to complete projects	like to start projects
goal-oriented	process-oriented
more structured	more easygoing
like things settled and decided	like things open and spontaneous

In the MBTI system, the word Judging does not mean judgmental or opinionated. In this context it simply means that people with a preference for Judging like to get decisions made as early as possible. They feel more comfortable when issues are resolved and plans are made and they prefer a structured and orderly lifestyle. They like to live in an organized and planned way. Until a decision has been reached about something they feel uneasy. It's not that all Judgers enjoy making decisions; it is more that they dislike leaving things open-ended and incomplete. They want to get things done and off their minds. They feel better knowing what time frames they have to work with. Commitments are seen as final and definite. They may have difficulty adapting to schedule changes and they can find it stressful when new information conflicts with or undoes decisions that have already been made.

Those who have a prefer-ence for Perceiving like to gather more information be-fore having to make deci-sions, and they like keeping their options open as long as possible. In the MBTI system, Perceiving does not mean perceptive or insightful. It simply means that Perceiv-ers are comfortable leaving

things unplanned or undecided; after all, something more interesting might come up in the meantime. Making decisions can be stressful for Perceiving types because, once the decision is made, all other choices are closed. They don't want to be tied down to their own or others' plans, schedules, or commitments. Going with the flow and letting life happen is much more appealing to them. They're flexible and adaptable, able to tolerate ambiguity, and are not bothered by things being up in the air. Commitments are seen as changeable and negotiable. If an unforseen event occurs, they enjoy improvising to adapt to the changes.

Both Judging and Perceiving have their challenges. Those who have a preference for Judging are so eager to make decisions that they may close off information-gathering too

quickly and miss important points. Those who prefer Perceiving may put off making decisions for too long while they keep gathering information; the time to act comes and goes and they miss out on something they wanted.

Judgers and Perceivers have been known to drive each other crazy. Perceivers can feel boxed in and pressured by a Judger's need for plans and orderly surroundings. Judgers can feel anxious and strung out by a Perceiver's tendency to leave things unplanned and scattered about.

As with the other preference pairs, if these two different ways of being are appreci-

ated and understood, they can benefit from each other's style. Those who prefer Judging would do well to learn to relax and go with the flow more, and those who prefer Perceiving can learn to be more organized and follow through on things.

How to get along with Judgers

- Appreciate their ability to be organized and efficient, to make decisions, and to bring things to completion.
- Respect their need to know "the plan." Try to agree to at least some part of a schedule or time frame.
- When you make a plan with them, honor your commitment and show your respect by being on time.
- Judging types like order. Be mindful of that by remembering to put things where they belong in their houses and to avoid leaving your things lying around.

How to get along with Perceivers

- Appreciate their flexibility and relaxed way of doing things.
- When a decision is needed, allow them time to ask questions and discuss options. If necessary, get an agreement on when they'll let you know their decision.
- Try not to impose unnecessary schedules or commitments on them.
- Let them know when it's *really* important that they follow through with something.

Suggestions for Judgers

I gave my life to learning how to live. Now that I have it all organized . . .
it's just about over.
—SANDRA HOCHMAN

- Try to be patient with people who take more time to make decisions than you do.
- Stop "doing" and take time to relax. Learn to let things be.
- Beware of making decisions too hastily and remember that it's okay to change your mind.
- Remember to apply your need for closure on yourself, not on others! Keep in mind that too much structured and planned time can be stressful to Perceivers.

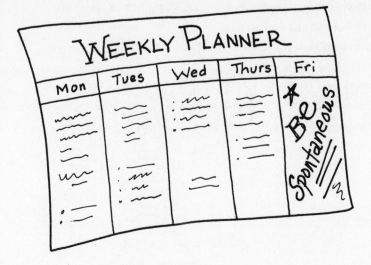

- Be open to doing some things on impulse. Schedule time to do something un-planned.
- Stop "doing" and take time to relax. Learn to let things be.
- Take a totally unplanned vacation. Go to the airport and get on whatever flight you can.
- Invite people over for dinner at the last minute. See if you can tolerate the lack of plan-ning.

Suggestions for Perceivers

I am one of those who never knows the direction of my journey
until I have almost arrived.
—Anna Louise Strong

- Be respectful of meeting deadlines. Keep your promises and commitments. Become aware of the effect on others of last-minute cancellations or showing up late.
- Find a job that allows for spontaneity and flexibility. If you have a job with a lot of deadlines, be sure to create plenty of unstructured time in the evenings and weekends.
- If you're living with a Judger, try to keep certain areas in your environment as struc-tured as possible.
- Honor your need for generat-ing new options but keep in mind that open-ended plans and surprises can be stressful to Judgers.

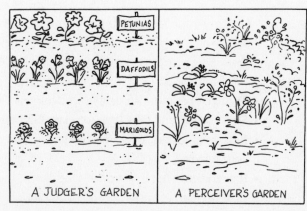

- Make a short list each day of what things you'd like to finish. Complete at least one thing per day and reward yourself when it's done.
- Ask a friend who is both patient and well organized to help you prioritize your goals for a week. Repeat it next week.
- Practice focusing on closure and follow-through rather than continually considering new options.

The absence of alternatives clears the mind
marvelously.
—HENRY KISSINGER

Now that you've read about Judging and Perceiving you probably have a good idea of what your preference is. If not, guess for now.

I think my preference is:

(J) _____   (P) _____

Turn to page 40 and write J or P in the fourth box to complete your four-letter type. Remember, if your scores are close, you can write both down and decide which is more accurate once you're learned more.

Chapter 7

How to Find Your Type

FINDING YOUR TYPE

The combination of your four preferences equals your type. Look at what you wrote in the boxes on the following page. These letters make up your type. If you had clear scores on all four preferences, you may have already found your type. Read its brief description on the chart starting on page 44 and see if it fits. If it does, then go on to Part II to learn more about what your temperament and type mean to you in different aspects of your life.

It is not uncommon to have close scores on one or two preference pairs. If this is the case you will have a few estimates of the preferences that make up your type. For example, you may have scored close on S and N, but have clear scores for E, F, and J. This means you are probably an ESFJ or ENFJ. Write down all your possible preference combinations. Turn to the charts on pages 44 to 47 and read the brief descriptions of your possible types to see which suits you best. Do they sound like you? Eliminate the ones that don't resemble you. On the same chart, read the brief temperament descriptions that your type(s) fall under.

For some people, finding their temperament first makes it easier. Reading the temperament descriptions will give you a broad overview. Since there are only four of them, once you become clear on your temperament, it is easier to narrow down your type.

When people find their correct temperament and type, they are surprised at how accurately the profiles describe them. If you get that "Wow, this is really me!" feeling or re-

E or I   S or N   T or F   J or P

sponse, you have most likely found your match. If it sounds only somewhat like you, then you probably have not identified your type yet.

Keep in mind, however, that not every word will describe you completely. People of the same type and temperament will have a lot in common, but we are all unique individuals. If there are statements in the descriptions that are absolutely not you, that is usually an indication that one of your preference letters is off.

If any of your preference pairs are still unclear, you may want to go over the Inventories again. Finding your type is like a treasure hunt.

Why It Might Be Hard to Find Your Type.

- If you felt pressured while growing up to behave in certain ways that were not your true style, you may have scored the statements based on how you think you should be rather than on what your true nature is. You might want to go back over the statements and ask yourself, "Is this really how I am, or is this how someone told me to be?"
- You may feel pressured by society's standards to be other than your natural self. For example, in the United States, Extraverting is the style of the majority. Introverting types may come up with a higher score on Extraverting if they think that is the better or the right way to be.
- If you are a female with a preference for Thinking or a male with a preference for Feeling, this is the opposite of the social norm in most cultures. It can affect how you answered the T and F Inventory.
- You might have arrived at a time in your life when you are focusing on developing some of your opposite preferences. For example, if you have a natural preference for leaving things open-ended and unstructured (Perceiving), but are wanting to become more organized and decisive (Judging), this can influence your score.
- Your work or career might require skills which are not your true style. For example, if you like being inventive and coming up with new possibilities for the future (iNtuiting), and your job requires routine, detail, or factual work (Sensing), this can influence your score.

If you are still having trouble identifying your type, keep track of your behavior for a few weeks. Observe yourself to see what you do naturally. Notice your choices, natural inclinations, and comforts in different situations. Talk to others about how they see you. You can also read some of the books suggested in the Resource section and/or take a workshop on types. You can take the Myers-Briggs Type Indicator (MBTI) and have it interpreted by a qualified professional. There are 126 questions on the standard form of the Indicator, and you may be able to get a clearer idea of your true preferences, if they are not obvious after reading this book.

For some people, even the long form of the MBTI (166 questions) is not enough to clearly distinguish their preferences. There is nothing wrong with being confused or uncertain on some or even all of the preference pairs. We simply invite you to try out this system for looking at personality type and style. Continue to observe, read, and ask questions about your true preferences. The rewards will be well worth your time.

A Brief Description of the 16 Myers-Briggs Types

Sensing Judging Types (SJ): Duty Seekers

SJs are motivated by a need to be useful and of service. they like to stick to the standard ways of doing things and value the traditions, customs, and laws of society.

ESTJ	ESFJ
Outgoing, energetic, and dependable. Efficient, organized, and decisive. Likes administrating and being in charge. Excellent at organizing and deciding policies and procedures. Assertive, outspoken, and direct. Focuses on solving problems. Responsible, hardworking, and goal-oriented. Consistent, pragmatic, and logical.	Enthusiastic, sociable, and engaging. Likes to be needed and appreciated. Personable, sympathetic, and cooperative. Like being helpful, active in service organizations. Trustworthy, loyal, and responsible. Values harmony and shows love in practical ways.
ISTJ	ISFJ
Reserved, persevering, loyal, and careful. Systematic, organized, and focused on the facts. Hardworking, thorough, and good at follow-through. Down-to-earth, pragmatic, and trustworthy. Honor their commitments. Do what is "right" and expect the same of others. Calm and consistent in crisis.	Conscientious, trustworthy, and cooperative. Loyal, dependable, and self-disciplined. Strong work ethic, completes tasks on time. Excellent memory for details. Quietly friendly, thoughtful, and reserved. Often works behind the scenes helping others. Modest and unassuming. Warm, tactful, and gentle.

Sensing Perceiving Types (SP): Action Seekers

SPs are motivated by a need for freedom and action. They value and enjoy living in the here and now.

ESTP Likes risk, challenge, and adventure. Energetic and constantly on the go. Lives life to the fullest. Alert, confident, and persuasive. Can be outrageous, direct, and impulsive. Competent, resourceful, and responds well to crises. Realistic, pragmatic, and matter-of-fact. Skillful negotiator.	**ESFP** Caring, generous, cooperative, and enjoys helping others. Friendly, gregarious, energetic, vivacious, and charming. Often the life of the party. Tolerant and accepting of self and others. Has practical common sense. Accentuates the positive. Enjoys new experiences and has zest for life.
ISTP Prefers action to conversation. Likes adventure and challenge. Does well in crisis. Enjoys working with tools, machines, and anything requiring hands-on skills. Resourceful, independent, and self-determined. Logical, realistic, and practical. Reserved, detached, curious observer. Storehouses of information and facts.	**ISFP** Gentle, loyal, and compassionate. Appears reserved and unassuming. Quietly does things for others. Patient, accepting, and nonjudgmental. Has a live-and-let-live attitude. Sensitive to conflicts and disagreement. Has little need to dominate or control others.

Intuiting Thinking Types (NT): Knowledge Seekers

NTs are motivated by a need to understand the world around them. They value competency and the powers of the mind.

ENTJ Confident leader who likes to be in charge. Decisive and ambitious. Likes intellectual exchange. Ingenious and resourceful in solving complex problems. Innovative, analytical, and logical. Self-determined and independent. Aspires to be the best at whatever (s)he does.	**ENTP** Outspoken and thrives on challenge and debate. Enthusiastic, charming, gregarious, and witty. Values freedom and independence. Innovative, enterprising, and resourceful. Spontaneous and impulsive. Risk-taker who is alert to all possibilities. Inquisitive and curious.
INTJ Independent and individualistic. Has great insight and vision. Skilled in creating theories and systems. Drives self and others toward goals and self-improvement. Ingenious and creative problem-solver. Organized, determined, and good at follow-through. Responsible, reserved, and private.	**INTP** Analytical and brilliant. Conceptual problem-solver and original thinker. Idiosyncratic and nonconforming. Values precision in thought and language. Notices inconsistencies, contradictions, and logical flaws in others' thinking. Independent, curious, and insightful. Private, aloof, and introspective.

INTUITING FEELING TYPES: (NF) IDEAL SEEKERS

NFs are motivated by a need to understand themselves and others. They value authenticity and integrity and strive for an ideal world.

ENFJ	ENFP
Friendly, charming, enthusiastic, and socially active. Persuasive speaker and inspiring, charismatic leader who motivates others. Empathic, warm, helpful, and supportive. Can idealize people and relationships. Responsible, conscientious, and goal-oriented. Diplomatic and good at promoting harmony.	Warm-spirited, helpful, accepting, and compassionate. Full of enthusiasm and new ideas. Values freedom and autonomy. Good at communicating and inspiring action. Creative, spontaneous, positive, and fun-loving. Individualistic, insightful, and perceptive.
INFJ	**INFP**
Sensitive, deep, and sometimes mystical. Single-minded regarding personal values and convictions. Has a rich inner life, and values personal integrity. Creative, original, and idealistic. Reserved, gentle, and compassionate. Enjoys solitude, yet has a strong need for harmony. Conscientious, determined, and persevering.	Devoted, compassionate, open-minded, and gentle. Dislikes rules, orders, schedules, and deadlines. Likes learning and being absorbed in own projects. Has passionate convictions, and drive for ideals. Sets high standards for self. Idealistic, sensitive, and creative. Can be reserved and contemplative.

Part II

Temperaments and Types

Chapter 8

An Introduction to Temperament

Having discovered your four basic preferences, you can now go on and figure out your temperament. Temperament can be described as a pattern of characteristic behaviors that reflect a person's natural disposition. It affects the way he sees the world, what he values and believes, and how he thinks, acts, and feels. People of the same temperament have similar core values, and they have many characteristics in common. Since temperament is inborn, and not acquired, a consistency of actions and behaviors can be observed from a very early age, even before the events of life imprint themselves on the person's psyche.

Temperament defines what we need and value and what we hunger for. These needs, values, and desires will determine our actions and behaviors. Studying temperament can be very useful because when we know what someone's temperament is, we can have a good idea as to what they will do in most situations most of the time.

The idea that people fall into four basic categories of temperament is not new. Four basic temperaments have been observed over many centuries by people from diverse cultures, and have been given many different names over the years. While Myers and Briggs did not set out to describe temperaments, their description of the sixteen personality types was found to fit neatly into the four historical temperaments which David Keirsey was studying.

In the Myers-Briggs system, the four temperament themes are called:

SJ—Sensing Judging
SP—Sensing Perceiving
NT—iNtuiting Thinking
NF—iNtuiting Feeling.

Understanding the four temperaments makes it easier to grasp the sixteen personality types. The temperament themes provide a framework for viewing the personality types since they cluster in patterns. For example, the SJ temperament is the root of the ESTJ, ISTJ, ESFJ, and ISFJ types. If you understand the SJ temperament as a whole, it will be easy to comprehend the basic motivations and values of all four of these personality types.

Sensing Judging Types (SJ): Duty Seekers

SJs are motivated by a need to be responsible in whatever social group they are in, whether it be the family, the workplace, or the community. They value tradition.
The four SJ types: ESTJ   ESFJ   ISTJ   ISFJ.

Sensing Perceiving Types (SP): Action Seekers

SPs are motivated by a need for freedom and need to act. They value living in the moment.
The four SP types: ESTP   ESFP   ISTP   ISFP.

iNtuiting Thinking Types (NT): Knowledge Seekers

NTs are motivated by a need for knowledge and competency. They value the theoretical and the powers of the mind.
The four NT types: ENTJ   ENTP   INTJ   INTP.

iNtuiting Feeling Types (NF): Ideal Seekers

NFs are motivated by a need to understand themselves and others. They value authenticity and integrity and strive for an ideal world.
The four NF types: ENFJ   ENFP   INFJ   INFP.

Chapter 9

Duty Seekers: The SJ Temperament and the Four SJ Types:
ESTJ   ESFJ   ISTJ   ISFJ

S: focuses on facts and reality.

J: wants things settled and decided.

SJs, at their best, are reliable, organized, focused on the task at hand, conscientious, and hardworking.

SJs, at their worst, are judgmental, controlling, inflexible, and close-minded.

Sensing Judging types are realistic, practical, and responsible, and they like to stick to standard ways of doing things. The traditions, customs, and laws of society are respected and honored, giving them a sense of safety, stability, and belonging. Feeling useful and needed is important to them, and they seek out duties and responsibilities. Being of service and making things run the way they should gives them satisfaction. Consequently, SJs have high expectations of themselves and others.

At work, SJs like to be fully in charge of their area of responsibility. They want to be useful and have difficulty refusing to take on extra assignments. Their attitude is "If I don't do it, who will?" They have a strong work ethic and believe that everyone can make something of themselves if they just work hard enough.

SJs want to contribute to the institutions they serve and they bring stability to an organization. They like jobs where performance is judged by established rules and explicitly stated criteria. They pay attention to an organization's hierarchy, have respect for the chain of command, and rely on stated policies and standard operating procedures. Their natural resistance to change can be reduced once they understand the rationale behind the change. In order to accept new ideas, they need to see the practical applications and benefits. Their approach to problem-solving is to apply past experience and follow the rules. They are usually good with facts and figures and precise with data, and they pay attention to detail. They can be sticklers for accuracy. They have a good sense of time and a realistic idea of how long it will take to complete a task.

They generally don't like surprises, and have a gift for anticipating problems that might disrupt their stability. Such potential problems get addressed early by the SJ. SJs have a tendency to make decisions too quickly without considering possible options. They are famous for having a good grasp of "common sense" in whatever they do. Unfortunately, they sometimes have a hard time seeing beyond their common sense to consider the suggestions of others.

SJs are loyal and faithful partners and they take their personal commitments and obligations seriously. They often feel more comfortable being the givers or caretakers than being the receivers. They tend to feel at ease in the traditional roles of provider or homemaker. When not appreciated, they can feel bitter and hurt, but they have difficulty expressing it. SJs can be pessimistic and worry excessively and think people who don't worry are irresponsible.

> *My mother always phones me and asks, "Is everything all wrong?"*
> —RICHARD LEWIS

When stressed, SJs can be pessimistic and see no way out of difficult situations. They tend to imagine worst-case scenarios rather than positive possibilities. They like to anticipate bad news and are generally prepared for setbacks and unpredictable events which they believe are bound to occur. At work they are often put in charge of disaster planning. They save their money and are willing to make sacrifices in the present for the sake of future security.

SJs provide an ordered and predictable environment for their children. They may find it difficult to allow their children independence and self-expression. Commitment to family life is seen as a responsibility and breaking family rules is seen as disloyalty. SJs sometimes instill guilt in their children when they don't meet their expectations.

SJ parents want their children to have the "proper" social attitudes and to obey the rules of society. SJs tend to place importance on grades, college, and traditional education, and they encourage practical careers.

As children and teens SJs are reliable and conscientious, and they try to please adults. They become very responsible starting at an early age and can act like a parent toward other children, or even toward their own parents! They thrive in an organized environment where there are clearly defined rules and routines. They prefer subjects that deal with facts and have practical application such as history, geography, civics, biology, math, spelling, typing, computers, or business. They like to participate in school activities and feel a sense of belonging.

How to get along with SJs

- Express regret if you have done something wrong. They like to hear "I'm sorry." It sets the world right for them.
- Appreciate their thoroughness, industriousness, loyalty, and willingness to take responsibility and handle the practical details.
- Try to have things run smoothly and efficiently. SJs dislike confusion, delays, and waste.
- Honor your commitments in order to win their trust and loyalty.
- Don't take advantage of their tendency to take on extra responsibilities.
- Respect their sense of tradition and social order.
- Be specific and practical. SJs value common sense and may be impatient with vague information, theories, or abstract thinking.
- Don't try to force them into new ways of doing things. Be understanding about their resistance to change.

Tips for SJs

- Avoid getting stuck in ruts. Just because it's the way you've always done it doesn't mean it's the only way.
- Beware of wanting too much control and giving orders laced with "shoulds."

- Remember that there is more than one right way to live. Develop the "to each his own" attitude.
- Learn to be tolerant of new ideas and theories—try some on for size!
- Don't rule out options too quickly because you consider them unrealistic. Practice using your intuition, playing with your imagination; learn to trust your dreams and hunches.
- Enjoy the moment for what it is, not for how you can make use of it, or how you can improve it.
- Allow the more spontaneous and free sides of your personality to develop and to have expression.
- Learn to ask for help and to delegate work to others. Don't try to do it all at the expense of becoming exhausted, resentful, ill, or depressed.

- Make time for fun.
- Realize that you can be supportive of others without doing things for them.
- Become aware of your own values. Ask yourself, "What is my life really about?" "What do I want to do with the rest of it?" (especially at midlife).

Now that you have an understanding of the SJ temperament it will be easier to learn about the four SJ types.

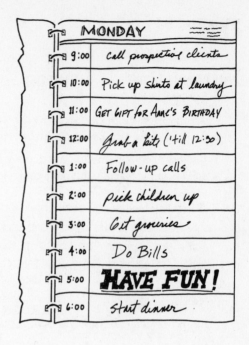

MONDAY

9:00 — Call prospective clients
10:00 — Pick up shirts at laundry
11:00 — GET GIFT FOR ANNE'S BIRTHDAY
12:00 — Grab a bite ('till 12:30)
1:00 — Follow-up calls
2:00 — pick children up
3:00 — Get groceries
4:00 — Do Bills
5:00 — HAVE FUN!
6:00 — Start dinner

ESTJ

Extraverting   Sensing   Thinking   Judging

E: is energized by the external world.
S: focuses on facts and reality.
T: makes objective, impersonal decisions.
J: wants things settled and decided.

ESTJs relish having responsibilities and controlling whatever is in their domain. They like being in charge. They are good at making objective decisions and focusing on their own or the organization's goals. ESTJs meet challenges head-on and know how to get things accomplished. They have opinions about everything, and are rarely at a loss for words.

> I don't believe in that "no comment" business. I always have a comment.
> —MARTHA MITCHELL

ESTJs at Work

- Excel at organizing procedures, policies, and activities.
- Use time and resources effectively to achieve immediate, tangible results.

> A team effort is a lot of people doing what I say.
> —MICHAEL WINNER

- Focus on resolving problems, reaching conclusions, and moving on.
- Expect others to demonstrate competency, effort, and follow-through.
- Are good at seeing what is illogical, inconsistent, impractical, or inefficient.
- Are willing to take calculated risks after careful thought.
- Like a stable, predictable environment, but one that has a variety of people.
- At their best, are tough and firm, but fair.
- Can be rigid, demanding, and impatient with those who don't follow procedures or pay attention to important details.
- Respect those who stand up to them, as long as they have the facts, know the rules, and are willing to take responsibility for their actions.

- Tend to be workaholics
  and drive themselves and
  others very hard.
- Can run people over in
  their effort to reach their
  goals.

Typical Occupations

Many different careers are suitable for ESTJs. The following is a list of some occupations that have proven to be satisfying for many ESTJs.

administrator	insurance agent
attorney	manager
auditor	mechanic
bank officer	military personnel or officer
computer programmer	physician
construction worker	police officer
dentist	real-estate broker
electrician	sales representative
engineer	stockbroker
financial manager	supervisor
general contractor	teacher
government worker	

ESTJs in Relationships

- Like being entrusted with responsibilities and playing the role of advisor.
- Are willing to make sacrifices in order to honor their commitments.
- Can be entertaining and fun and have a good time when their work is done.
- Enjoy active pursuits with their family and friends.
- May impose structure, order, and their will on everyone; are convinced that their way is best.

I may have my faults, but being wrong ain't one of them.
—JIMMY HOFFA

- Are direct, honest, straightforward, and often blunt.
- Can be impatient and abrupt and may have difficulty listening to others' points of view.
- May have trouble understanding their own and others emotions.
- Have a tough exterior but can be tender with those they trust.
- Like to provide possessions and security for their family's well-being.
- Define their success and happiness by what they do in the outer world.

Leisure

ESTJs like to spend their free time in ways that are productive. They get things done. Activities that combine work with socializing, such as playing racketball or golf with business associates, are their favorites. Many ESTJs are in charge of community service organizations and volunteer activities. They will gladly spend their time on causes they believe in. They also enjoy socializing and joking around with family and friends.

Suggestions for ESTJs

Think for yourselves and let others enjoy the privilege to do so too.
—Voltaire

- Listen to the other person's point of view.
- Work at negotiating solutions that are win-win.
- Value and acknowledge the efforts of others.
- Make it a rule to mention what is well done, not merely what needs correcting.
- Surround yourself with people who respect your direct approach and are not intimidated by you.
- Beware of driving others as hard as you drive yourself.
- Set realistic limits for yourself and others and learn what "good enough" means.

- Refrain from telling others what they should and shouldn't do. Do not assume that you know what's best.
- Expand your sense of self to include more than what you do or produce.
- Become aware of your hurt and fear, not just your anger.
- Learn ways to control your temper and to restrain yourself when you are about to react impatiently. Leave the room or the house until you cool down.
- Learn to let go of control and to relax. Take a vacation and leave all your work at home.

- Appreciate your strengths—realism, practicality, objectiveness, logic, responsibility, decisiveness, dependability, consistency, organizational ability.

ESFJ
Extraverting Sensing Feeling Judging

E: is energized by the outer world.

S: focuses on facts and reality.

F: decides according to personal values.

J: wants things settled and decided.

ESFJs are warmhearted, outgoing, and friendly. They are highly sociable and they get restless when isolated from others. They thrive on being needed and appreciated and are often more attuned to others' needs than to their own. ESFJs follow social standards, and are concerned about their place in society. They have many shoulds and should nots for themselves and others.

ESFJs at Work

- Are conscientious, diligent, organized, and they get the job done.
- Like their work to be scheduled and routinized.
- Are good at following through on details and making sure things run efficiently and smoothly.
- Are good team players; they like to work in a congenial atmosphere and want everyone at work to be their friend.
- Want decisions made early, but do not need to make all the decisions themselves.
- Are cooperative, service-oriented, and want to provide practical and tangible help to others.
- Dislike dealing with problems on a theoretical or philosophical basis.
- Are attentive and warm when dealing with people.
- Are very outgoing and lean toward occupations involving people.
- Like working in a conflict-free environment, helping people to work harmoniously toward a common goal.
- Do not seek leadership positions but make important contributions when they hold such positions.
- Have high regard for authority and believe others ought to honor authorities as well.

Typical Occupations

Many different careers are suitable for ESFJs. The following is a list of some occupations that have proven to be satisfying for many ESFJs.

banker	nurse
bookkeeper	office manager
caterer	physical therapist
cleaning service worker	real-estate agent
coach	religious worker
counselor	restaurant worker
dental or medical assistant	retail salesperson
flight attendant	secretary
hairstylist	social worker
health care worker	speech pathologist
human resources trainer	teacher
interior decorator	telemarketer
merchandise planner	

ESFJs in Relationships

A good heart is better than all the heads in the world.
—EDWARD BULWER-LYTTON

- Are compassionate, sympathetic, and considerate.
- Tend to be very talkative; are comfortable chatting with just about anyone.

- Focus on people's best qualities and tend to idealize those whom they admire.
- Value harmony and try to not offend or disappoint anyone.
- Can be overly ingratiating and appear insincere and phony.
- Like a lot of personal attention, validation, and

praise for all that they do for others.

- Are conscious of appearances and respect social status; they may compare their possessions with others and try to "keep up with the Joneses."

- Thrive on being needed but can feel overburdened and stressed from taking care of others.

- Can become depressed and melancholy, or spiteful and blaming, if they feel criticized or unappreciated for all they have done.

- Like to keep traditions alive and hold on to their nostalgic memories.

- Can be rigid, opinionated, and critical of those who don't share their view or look at things in the same way.

Leisure

ESFJs lead very busy lives. They are gracious hosts and hostesses and like to make people feel comfortable and welcome. Their parties are well planned and often lavishly put together. ESFJs devote time and energy to social and community organizations that they respect. Spending time with their family and friends is also very important.

MON	TUES	WED	THURS	FRI	SAT
Volunteer work	Babysit	Volunteer Work	Baby sit	10:00 AM Tennis	9:00— Rummage Sale 6:00— Goldsmiths for dinner
help Sally	Shop Chinese cooking class	Buy gifts for Ann's birthday	DO PAPERWORK	pick up Dan's shirts Call Children	SUN
Choral Group	Babysit	PTA Night	5:00— Aerobics Class	Movies with the Bergs	Birthday Party for Joan

Suggestions for ESFJs

- Try not to avoid conflict by becoming accommodating or ingratiating, or by sweeping problems under the rug.

I don't know the key to success, but the key to failure is trying to please everybody.
—BILL COSBY

- Focus on what you want to do rather than on what you should do. Being selfish is not always a sin.
- Avoid the tendency to jump in and try to fix a situation as fast as possible. Conflict and difficulties are not necessarily bad—they can help everyone grow and change.
- Slow down your pace. Free up time for reflection and for the activities that might ground and focus you, such as crafts, needlework, or woodwork.
- Notice the difference between your real feelings and the ones you put on because they seem like appropriate ones to have.
- Be brief and businesslike when it is called for.
- Avoid any occupation where your friendly, happy, outgoing nature will not be appreciated.
- Ask others if they want your help or advice before offering it.

- Avoid being manipulative in order to get what you want. Learn to be more direct. It's okay to ask for what you need.
- Avoid blaming and guilt-tripping others when your expectations are not met or when you feel taken for granted.
- Learn to trust yourself rather than always seeking answers from outside authorities.
- Appreciate your strengths—being conscientious, responsible, nurturing, friendly, loyal, sympathetic, and persevering.

ISTJ
Introverting   Sensing   Thinking   Judging

I: is energized by their internal world.

S: focuses on facts and reality.

T: decides according to objective, logical principles.

J: wants things settled and decided.

ISTJs are extremely stable, responsible, and dependable. They are outwardly composed, steady, and matter-of-fact. ISTJs are people of few words, who are private and self-contained. Being punctual, precise, fastidious, and orderly are qualities they expect of themselves and others. They have an ability to concentrate well and are difficult to distract.

ISTJs at Work

- Are good at remembering facts and figures; they have an internal filing system that stores detailed, objective information.
- Value thoroughness and accuracy and like to see concrete, tangible results.
- Go over their work with a fine-toothed comb to be sure that nothing is overlooked.
- Can be overly detail-oriented; are devoted hard workers.

- Work better with machines, facts, and numbers than with people.
- Like to work alone; dislike distractions and disruptions.
- Expect rules and orders to be followed and have little tolerance for those who deviate.
- Tolerate the procedures and regulations of an institution but can be impatient with the individuals.
- Dislike apathy, idleness, and disorganization; see easygoing laid-back types as undisciplined and unmotivated.
- Have a tendency to be rigid and inflexible, and to "go by the book."
- Dislike occupations where dress, surroundings, and surface appearances are important.

Beware of all enterprises that require new clothes.
—HENRY DAVID THOREAU

- Earn promotions by steady hard work, mastering the necessary skills and knowledge, and being loyal to the organization.

Typical Occupations

Many different careers are suitable to ISTJs. The following is a list of some occupations that have proven to be satisfying for many ISTJs.

accountant	librarian
administrator	manager
auditor	mechanic
banker	medical technician
cleaning service worker	military personnel
computer programmer	optician
construction worker	optometrist
contractor	paralegal
dentist	pharmacist
detective	physician
electrician	police officer
engineer	stockbroker
government worker	teacher
insurance agent	technician
lawyer	underwriter

ISTJs in Relationships

- Make extremely loyal mates and honor their commitments. Their word is their bond and you can count on it.
- Show love through doing practical things and being loyal and dependable. "Actions speak louder than words."
- May have difficulty expressing feelings of warmth and tenderness to loved ones, even though their affections often run very deep.
- Have a dry understated wit.
- Can be outgoing and socially adept, but on a personal level they are sometimes inaccessible.
- Are modest, unassuming, and down-to-earth.
- Are extremely practical and pragmatic.

- Are resistant to change and are not easily swayed from their opinions or direction.
- Can be unaware of their own and others' emotions and have difficulty understanding needs that differ from their own.
- Can make quick critical judgments of others.
- Tend to be frugal and don't like to waste their hard-earned money on frivolities.

The safest way to double your money is to fold it over once and
put it in your pocket.
—Kin Hubbard

Leisure

ISTJs tend to find it hard to relax as they may view the things that bring them joy as nonproductive. They like to focus on activities that have a purpose and a concrete outcome. For example, tinkering with a complex machine or computer program will be more fun if they fix or master it. They also enjoy being in nature and will notice many details about their surroundings. They prefer simplicity to status and extravagance, preferring entertainment and dining that is economical and unpretentious.

> *Stained glass, engraved glass, frosted glass; give me plain glass.*
> —JOHN FOWLES

Suggestions for ISTJs

- Learn to negotiate and try to see things from other perspectives.
- Make it a rule to say "I love you" at least once a week.

- Avoid being overly cautious and rigid in your thinking. Be open to seeing that there is not just one right way of doing things.
- Avoid having conversations that can only end in win-lose propositions.
- Do something impulsive now and then. Be lazy and goof off once in a while.
- Share your humorous thoughts more often.
- Pay attention to your own and others' emotions; develop the habit of putting words to the feelings you have.

- Listen for data about the needs and feelings of others.
- Make an extra effort to express appreciation to others, even for the small things they do.
- Take time for relaxation and play. Don't forget to use your allotted vacation time.

- Appreciate your strengths of being diligent, practical, precise, logical, dependable, dutiful, sensible, orderly, steady, thorough, hardworking, and persevering.

ISFJ
Introverting   Sensing   Feeling   Judging

I: is energized by their internal world.
S: focuses on facts and reality.
F: decides according to personal values.
J: wants things settled and decided.

ISFJs are extremely dependable, loyal, and committed. They are quiet, reserved, modest, and unassuming. ISFJs like to be of service and they go to great lengths to be helpful. They behave as they are supposed to and don't question the established way of doing things. ISFJs are down-to-earth, practical, conscientious, and painstakingly diligent.

ISFJs at Work

- Pay meticulous attention to detail and are accurate and thorough with facts.
- Try to do everything perfectly; small mistakes weigh heavily on them.
- Are persevering; will go to great lengths to get the job done.
- Show support and concern for subordinates and coworkers.
- Have trouble being direct, giving orders, or asking for help.

- Prefer to work behind the scenes; don't like to be in the limelight or public eye.
- Are adept with work that requires sequential, repeated procedures and like tasks where they can see tangible results.

- Select their priorities carefully and work out necessary steps in advance before beginning a new project.
- Like contributing to an institution they respect and being of service to people.
- Are highly self-determined and self-motivated.
- Have little need for supervision and do not ask others to do what they can do themselves.
- Like to work with a minimum of interruption and to focus on one project or person at a time.
- Are uncomfortable with lack of clear direction or uncertainty and dislike constant change.
- Respect authority and have trouble understanding those who don't.

Typical Occupations

Many different careers are suitable for ISFJs. The following is a list of some occupations that have proven to be satisfying for many ISFJs.

bookkeeper	optician
clerical supervisor	paralegal
computer operator	pharmacist
counselor	physical therapist
curator	probation officer
dental hygienist	religious educator
dietician	respiratory therapist
health service worker	retail owner
household worker	secretary
librarian	social worker
medical assistant	speech pathologist
nurse	teacher
office manager	veterinarian

ISFJs in Relationships

- Are kind, considerate, quietly friendly, and sensitive to what others are feeling.
- Express love through thoughtful attention to others' needs.
- Enjoy making life comfortable for their family and people who are important to them.
- Appear calm and poised and try to keep everything under control.
- Review events from a highly personal perspective and have a rich inner world.

- Can feel taken for granted and undervalued for what they give, but may keep their hurt and resentment to themselves.
- Can stay in relationships with irresponsible people out of a sense of duty, in order to feel needed.
- May keep their feelings and needs inside to avoid displeasing or disappointing others.
- Can readily spot insincerity and phoniness.
- Enjoy a focused and structured lifestyle which gives them a sense of identity, security, and direction.
- Can make quick critical judgments but are careful to not hurt others.
- May see only the negative possibilities and can become pessimistic.

Leisure

*Marcia was incredibly organized, obsessively neat . . . I mean,
she folded her underwear like origami.*
—LINDA BARNES

ISFJs focus on their physical surroundings and comforts. They enjoy their homes and like to keep things organized and tidy. They prefer low-key, planned activities and especially enjoy having time for their creative projects. They like being with family and close friends, having special dinners and traditional holiday gatherings. Relaxing can be hard for them as they feel they should always be doing something productive.

Suggestions for ISFJs

*"No" uttered from the deepest conviction is better and greater than a
"yes" merely uttered to please.*
—MAHATMA GANDHI

- Beware of rescuing irresponsible, needy people. Get help in ending inappropriate relationships and situations.
- Talk to yourself in nurturing and caring ways. Pat yourself on the back. Don't wait for someone else to tell you that you did well.
- Honor your need for time alone. Schedule time for fun and personally satisfying activities.

- Allow room for mistakes.
- Talk about your needs, desires, and problems with a trusted friend or counselor. Let others help you for a change.
- Take time to discover your direction, purpose, and goals. Make choices based on your inner values rather than on external authorities.
- Remember that there is no one right way to live. What counts is that you are satisfied.

- Beware of excessive worrying. Don't spend too much time focusing on worst-case scenarios.
- Avoid taking on extra work. Learn to say NO!

- Get mad once in a while. Unleash pent-up resentment through writing, talking, or hitting pillows. You may feel guilty but you may also find it refreshing.

- Do not underestimate yourself and your accomplishments. Talk about them.
- Appreciate your strengths—being realistic, practical, conscientious, sensitive, sympathetic, loyal, friendly, superdependable, and persevering.

Chapter 10

Action Seekers: The SP Temperament and the Four SP Types:
ESTP   ESFP   ISTP   ISFP

S: focuses on facts and reality.
P: wants things left open and flexible.

SPs at their best are optimistic, generous, fun-loving, adventurous, realistic, and adaptable.

SPs at their worst are hyperactive, impatient, impulsive, and scattered.

SPs enjoy life in the here and now. Freedom is highly valued, and they resist being restricted or controlled. They are spontaneous and trust their impulses to lead them in the right direction. They just want to live life and experience it; they don't need to understand it. SPs are optimistic. They trust that they can handle anything that comes up and recover well from setbacks. They are keen observers of the environment and they have a commonsense approach to problems.

At work, SPs are practical, pragmatic, and resourceful and want to do things that deliver results. They like to see the daily tangible product of their work. They collect data by observing and asking the right questions to get the information they need. Their observational strengths are focused on the specifics of the immediate present. SPs like to make work fun, and they want their careers to be exciting. They see work not as a means to an end, but as an opportunity to experience still more of what life has to offer.

DAVE ALWAYS RUNS THE BEST MEETINGS.

SPs like risk and challenge. They respond well to crisis, but can lose interest once the crisis is over. They want to take immediate action and dislike wasting time talking about policies and procedures. They are ingenious at solving immediate problems by plunging in and just doing it. Setting long-term, abstract goals is not a priority. They dislike laws, hierarchical order, and standard ways of doing things. They believe that rules and traditions are meant to be changed and adapted to the needs of the moment. Routine or overly structured work environments are draining. They like working with practical people who are interested in taking action. SPs like work that they call "real jobs" and it is more acceptable nowadays for women to hold these jobs as well.

SPs enjoy a partner who will share in their many experiences and adventures. They enjoy being with positive, upbeat people. They don't want to miss out on anything and they try to cram a lot into their lives. SPs like living the good life and are constantly making plans for fun-filled adventures. They have realistic expectations of themselves, others, and life, and they don't waste energy wishing things were different from what they are. They are open-minded and willing to compromise and negotiate. They love surprises, the unexpected, and thrive on last-minute changes. They take what people say at face value and are not interested in figuring out underlying motives

or hidden meanings. When information is too remote from their day-to-day life, they lose interest.

As parents SPs can be enthusiastic, playful, and expose their children to many adventures. They give their children freedom and autonomy and respect their individual wishes and desires. SPs want their children to do something practical with their lives and find work that they enjoy. They can be overly permissive, nondirective, and fail to provide consistency, discipline, or planning for the future.

As children and teens, SPs are often too busy doing activities and having fun to take time to sit down and study. They often jump from one thing to another, but can be involved in an activity for an extended period of time if it captures their attention. Their sense of accomplishment comes from "doing." These children tend to be risk-takers and usually leap before they look; they like immediate gratification.

SPs dislike long lectures and explanations and often shun intellectual pursuits. They'd much rather figure something out on their own than be told how to do it, especially if it means using their hands or bodies, as in sports or with crafts, machines, or music. They can have trouble concentrating on what others want them to focus on. An action-centered, hands-on curriculum works best. SPs like to learn subjects that are practical, relevant, and immediately rewarding.

SPs who have a strong Extraverting preference (ESTP, ESFP) are talkative, gregarious, and initiate activities with friends. SPs who have a strong Introverting preference (ISTP, ISFP) are more reserved and busy with their inner world of thoughts and private conversations. SP children's natural talents and abilities are often overlooked and undeveloped in schools that use traditional teaching methods and that are run primarily by SJs. SP children can underestimate themselves and suffer from low self-esteem as a result. They are sometimes labeled hyperactive, or as having Attention Deficit Disorder (ADD) because the sit-down, follow-directions, speak-when-spoken-to school structure goes against their nature. Some drop out and return to school only if they see that an education will be useful and practical in their lives.

How to get along with SPs

- Appreciate their enthusiasm, optimism, common sense, realism, and ability to deal with crisis.
- Join them in some of their many activities and adventures.
- Give them freedom. Don't try to box them in to too many schedules and routines.
- When making a request, give them choices and alternatives, then let go of your expectations. SPs want to do things in their own way, in their own time.
- Don't try to change them or tell them what to do.
- Avoid too much analyzing, processing of feelings, or discussing theories and abstractions.
- Don't overwhelm them with lots of issues. Pinpoint problems you're having and set aside a limited time to discuss them. Sometimes discussions while walking or doing some physical activity are the best.

Tips for SPs

- Develop persistence and follow-through in order to gain a sense of completion and accomplishment.
- Beware of your tendency to take shortcuts.
- Finish what you start and see your efforts pay off before you move on to new challenges.
- Avoid making too many quick decisions.
- Spend time considering what is important to you in order to become clear about your goals and priorities.

- Beware of the tendency to distract yourself with activity to avoid problems. Better to address issues as they come up than to let them accumulate.
- Remember the promises you made yesterday.

- Curb the impulse to deal only with immediate problems instead of the less exciting but nonetheless important ones.
- Learn to enjoy the deeper and quieter aspects of life, not just the highs and excitements.

Now that you have an understanding of the SP temperament, it will be easier to learn about the four SP types.

ESTP
Extraverting   Sensing   Thinking   Perceiving

E: is energized by the external world.

S: focuses on facts and reality.

T: decides according to objective, logical principles.

P: wants things left open and flexible.

ESTPs are confident, gregarious, and exciting. Being with people who share their interests and sense of fun and adventure is pleasurable for them. They have a charming, infectious manner, but can also be straightforward, assertive, and blunt. Their energy is boundless and they are constantly on the go. ESTPs like living on the edge and can be oblivious to consequences.

> *Moderation is a fatal thing: nothing succeeds like excess.*
> —OSCAR WILDE

ESTPs at Work

- Are resourceful, pragmatic, ready to deal with reality, and very results-oriented.
- Use logic in dealing head-on with concrete problems; get to the bottom of things quickly.
- Have a capacity for absorbing and remembering lots of facts.
- Like the pressure of pulling things together at the last minute; are motivated by tight deadlines.
- Are extremely cool under pressure.
- Are good at easing tense situations and pulling conflicting factions together.
- Can be driven and intense; seek recognition and success.
- Are competitive and tough-minded; thrive in crisis and chaos.
- Will play by the rules only if the rules help them do and get what they want. They pride themselves on being rebellious.
- Are persuasive and promote themselves well; easily find jobs through networking.
- Often have many projects going on at once.
- Enjoy high-energy, high-stress occupations which involve endurance, strength, and risk.

Typical Occupations

Many different careers are suitable for ESTPs. The following is a list of some occupations that have proven to be satisfying for many ESTPs.

attorney	management consultant
carpenter	mechanic
coach	military personnel
computer systems analyst	paramedic
construction worker	performer
contractor	police officer
detective	professional athlete
emergency medical technician	real-estate agent
engineer	sales representative
entrepreneur	stockbroker
farmer	technician
firefighter	transportation operative

ESTPs in Relationships

- Are independent and freedom-loving; want a great deal of latitude and dislike being controlled.
- Can easily feel trapped by pressure, obligation, and commitments.

- Are always on the lookout for some new adventure or experience.
- Are optimistic and don't spend much time in worry and regret.
- Know many people and get along well with diverse groups of people.

Anybody who goes to a psychiatrist ought to have his head examined.
—SAMUEL GOLDWYN

- Are not very interested in dealing with interpersonal or emotional issues.
- Like to impress potential mates with their charisma, success, and strength.
- Are extremely generous with material things but can forget to do the personal things that create intimacy and trust.
- Bring excitement and spontaneity to their relationships.
- Can be stimulated by conflict and like to be in the fray.
- Can be unpredictable; can do the opposite of what you expect and feel no need to justify their actions.

Leisure

It is better to wear out than to rust out.
—RICHARD CUMBERLAND

ESTPs like being center stage and enjoy telling stories and playing practical jokes. They like the good things in life and spend a lot of time socializing with their many friends and acquaintances. They seek risk-taking adventures such as mountain climbing, skiing, hunting, skydiving, racing, and surfing. Personal and intimate relationships are often less important to them than competition, activity, and adventure.

Suggestions for ESTPs

- If you want to gain the respect of others at work, be mindful of the standard ways of doing things.
- In order to gain more acceptance for your projects, develop a plan of action rather than always relying on improvisation.
- Resist the urge to deal only with the immediate exciting problems instead of the less exciting but important tasks.
- Beware of overwhelming others with your assertiveness and bluntness. Save some of your outrageous behavior for when you're with your outrageous friends.
- Try to be generous with the personal things that show you care.

- Remember to say "I love you" and give encouragement and praise.
- Avoid getting so involved in your projects and adventures that you forget about your friends and loved ones.
- Look beyond material pleasures to other things of more lasting value.

He who knows that enough is enough will always have enough.
—Lao-tzu, *Tao Te Ching*

- Consider how your actions impact yourself and others. Worry a little.
- Keep in mind that excitement, surprise, and variety are not always comforting for types who prefer more stability, consistency, and predictability.
- Learn to recognize and appreciate people's differences and to consider others in decision-making.
- Take the time to reflect on your experiences in order to see which ones are valuable, rewarding, and satisfying to you.
- Appreciate your strengths—being realistic, practical, resourceful, friendly, witty, clever, fun, adventurous, and pragmatic.

ESFP
Extraverting   Sensing   Feeling   Perceiving

E: is energized by the outer world.

S: focuses on facts and reality.

F: decides according to personal values.

P: wants things left open and flexible.

ESFPs are friendly, upbeat, witty, charming, and talkative. They value and nurture their relationships, giving generously without expecting anything in return. They are spontaneous, playful, and take delight in everything they do and see. People who share in their sense of fun and adventure are their favorite companions.

Years may wrinkle the skin, but to give up enthusiasm wrinkles the soul.
—SAMUEL ULLMAN

ESFPs at Work

- Like working in a lively and stimulating atmosphere with friendly, energetic people.
- Can be good at dealing with the public.
- Like variety and frequent change of tasks or jobs.
- Constantly scan the environment and quickly size up a situation.
- Are skillful at handling conflict; they have an ability to ease tension and help people work cooperatively.
- Are resourceful and use good common sense.
- Dislike hashing and rehashing information and possible solutions; want to get to the point and resolve issues quickly.
- Are good at motivating and including others in decision-making; promote teamwork.
- Enjoy careers where they can be of practical service to others.
- Often wait until the last minute to prepare and sometimes give follow-through a low priority.
- Can have problems knowing how long it will take to complete a task.

Typical Occupations

Many different careers are suitable for ESFPs. The following is a list of some occupations that have proven to be satisfying for many ESFPs.

animal groomer or trainer	physical therapist
athletic coach	police officer
designer	professional athlete
dietician or nutritionist	public relations specialist
fitness instructor	real-estate agent
flight attendant	recreation worker
fund-raiser	salesperson
medical assistant	social worker
merchandise planner	special events coordinator
musician	teacher
nurse	transportation operative
occupational therapist	travel agent
performer	veterinarian or assistant

ESFPs in Relationships

There is no personal charm so great as the charm of a cheerful temperament.
—Henry Van Dyke

- Are easygoing and accepting of themselves and others.
- Amuse and distract others from overly serious concerns; refuse to spread gloom and doom.

- Are enthusiastic, high-spirited, and have an upbeat energy.
- Like attention and seek affirmation and approval.
- See relationships as fun and don't necessarily need to have an intense, emotional connection.
- Are sympathetic to the suffering of others.

- Can overwhelm others with their generous show of love and gifts.
- Can be impulsive, impatient, and unpredictable.
- Prefer action to contemplation; may find it difficult to sit still or be alone.

Leisure

Too much of a good thing can be wonderful.
—MAE WEST

ESFPs turn everything into a fun-filled event. They like entertaining, especially big parties or gatherings, and

are good at getting things together at the last minute. Their homes are often filled with people. ESFPs enjoy the good things in life such as music, dance, food, drink, and amusements. They avoid being alone and like life to be a continual party of effortless abundance.

Suggestions for ESFPs

- Do not ignore troubling situations in hope that they will go away. Realize that positive thinking won't solve every problem. Allow negative feelings to emerge and get into the "dirt" when necessary.
- Avoid making snap decisions in crises that you may later regret.
- Be careful of getting so involved in all your activities that you forget about your responsibilities.
- Resist the urge to drop what you've started when a more interesting situation arises.
- Take time to digest and reflect on your experiences instead of just accumulating new ones.
- Beware of becoming overly focused on material things for happiness.
- Keep in mind that variety and excitement are not what all types crave. Don't tell people they're party poopers just because they're not like you.
- Take care of your health. Avoid overextending, overindulging, and excess stimulation.

- Avoid taking on so much at once that you end up feeling scattered, frazzled, and overextended.

WHAT SUE PACKS INTO A DAY WOULD BE ENOUGH TO FILL A WHOLE MONTH FOR MOST PEOPLE.

- Don't forget to spend time alone just to check in with yourself; listen to your inner voice.
- Become aware of your own values and goals in order to gain clarity about the larger meaning of your life.
- Appreciate your strengths—being warm, witty, accepting, adaptable, optimistic, adventurous, charming, generous, friendly, cooperative, and vivacious.

ISTP
Introverting   Sensing   Thinking   Perceiving

I: is energized by their internal world.
S: focuses on facts and reality.
T: decides according to objective, logical principles.
P: wants things left open and flexible.

ISTPs are quiet, curious onlookers who stand back and observe. They can be hard to figure out and remain a mystery to most people. They are independent and individualistic and do not behave in accordance with convention or others' expectations. ISTPs are action-oriented risk-takers who take pride in their ability to meet challenges. Their cool, dispassionate, and analytical reserve can make them appear slightly different from the other SP types.

ISTPs at Work

An ounce of action is worth a ton of theory.
—FRIEDRICH ENGELS

- Are focused on the tangible reality around them.
- Have a strong sense of timing; they deal with concrete problems expediently and don't waste effort on the unnecessary.
- Dislike ambiguity and listening to unnecessary details; prefer to get to the point of the issue so they can go to work on it.
- Enjoy trouble-shooting and like to solve problems in a systematic, logical, and efficient way.
- Tend to bypass rules, policies, and regulations when they get in the way of the results.
- See hierarchy and authority as unnecessary and can be extremely resistant to them.
- Dislike supervising or being supervised.
- Prefer to work alone unless it is with a colleague who has as much, or more, technical ability than they have.

- Tend to remain calm in a crisis.
- Are skilled masters of tools and operate them with amazing precision.
- Retain a great amount of detail and facts in areas that interest them and are quick and skillful at organizing data into a logical framework.
- Can easily become restless and bored at work that is not continually challenging.

Typical Occupations

Many different careers are suitable for ISTPs. The following is a list of some occupations that have proven to be satisfying for many ISTPs.

auditor	mechanic
carpenter	military personnel
coach or trainer	paralegal
computer programmer	paramedic
construction worker	police officer
dental or medical assistant	private investigator
economist	repairman
electrical technician	securities analyst
engineer	steelworker
farmer	surveyor
firefighter	technician
marine biologist	transportation operator

ISTPs in Relationships

Talk low, talk slow, and don't say too much.
—JOHN WAYNE

- Have little need for talking and socializing; prefer to communicate through action, rather than words.
- Show their love in practical, tangible ways by doing favors and fixing things.
- Are resistant to obligations, duties, or confining promises; can easily feel trapped by emotional commitment.
- Like to be with people who either share their interests or will give them freedom to do their own thing.
- Are often loners, but can be extremely loyal to those important to them.

92

- Can be unpredictable and challenging for other types to live with.
- May have difficulty with interpersonal skills and seem detached or uncaring to those who are not close to them.
- Can appear to be critical and insensitive because of their focus on facts and logic.

- Don't instigate conflicts, but won't shy away from them either. Like to be straightforward and direct.

Leisure

The spur of the moment is the essence of adventure.
—ANTONY ARMSTRONG-JONES

ISTPs like daring, dangerous, adrenaline-driven pursuits such as racing, hang gliding, rock climbing, skiing, or surfing. Many enjoy mastering competitive strategies to outmaneuver their opponents in sports. They avidly pursue their interests and activities and don't like to be bored. ISTPs can be extremely efficient in organizing their collections and hobbies but disorganized in areas where they have no interest.

Suggestions for ISTPs

- Take a break from immediate results by thinking about long-range goals and what you want for the future.

- Learn to consider that another's point of view has possibilities that you haven't thought of.
- Realize that people do things differently and that there are many ways of structuring life. Expand beyond black-and-white thinking.
- Mention points where you agree with another person before bringing up the places where you disagree.
- Point out the good things about others, not just the things to correct. When due, give an appreciative word of praise.
- Act on your affectionate impulses once in a while, letting others know they are important to you.
- Make time for your significant relationships.
- Learn ways to express your feelings and to achieve greater openness in communication. Share your insights more openly.
- Appreciate your strengths—being logical, spontaneous, practical, independent, adventurous, objective, realistic, and energetic.

ISFP
Introverting   Sensing   Feeling   Perceiving

I: is energized by their internal world.
S: focuses on facts and reality.
F: decides according to personal values.
P: wants things left open and flexible.

ISFPs are easygoing, likable, and have an attitude of live and let live. They are often quiet, reserved, and modest and don't call attention to themselves. ISFPs live in the present and appreciate the simple things in life. Harmonious relationships are important. They are loyal, gentle, compassionate, and often put others' needs before their own.

The luxury of doing good surpasses every other enjoyment.
—JOHN GAY

ISFPs at Work

- Are idealists and need to find work that is gratifying and consistent with their personal or inner values.
- Tend to have high inner standards of perfection.
- Are loyal and cooperative workers and can be highly motivated when their work contributes to something they care deeply about or believe in.
- Like to be useful and enjoy helping people develop practical skills.
- Are flexible and adaptable, and like working with people in a cooperative, egalitarian environment.
- Feel restricted by excessive rules, inflexible structure, and bureaucracy.
- Thrive in a supportive and affirming environment where there is little interpersonal conflict.
- Have little or no desire to control or compete; prefer to work behind the scenes.
- Can bring a certain sense of joy and quiet enthusiasm to the work environment.
- Deal with what is needed at the moment.
- Do well in emergency situations, bringing compassion to the situation.
- Can become overwhelmed by their own indecisiveness, lack of direction, and motivation. Organization can be a problem.

Typical Occupations

Many different careers are suitable for ISFPs. The following is a list of some occupations that have proven to be satisfying for many ISFPs.

artist

beautician

botanist

carpenter

clerical worker

computer operator

counselor

dancer

dental and medical assistant

designer

dietician or nutritionist

factory worker

food service worker

forester

gardener

geologist

marine biologist

mechanic

nurse

occupational therapist

optician

physical therapist

police officer

recreation leader

secretary

teacher

veterinarian or assistant

AN ISFP's WORST JOB.

ISFPs in Relationships

- Are nurturing, generous, unselfish, loyal, and kind.
- Are good listeners and are sympathetic to the needs of others.
- Can make difficult situations easier and often pull others through in hard times.
- Express affection through actions more than through words.
- Are keenly perceptive of others but tend to keep their observations to themselves.

- Appear relaxed and lighthearted but have an depth and complexity under their calm, quiet exterior.
- Tend to take criticism personally; retreat if hurt and will often blame themselves for others' actions and reactions.
- Can be overpowered by more controlling types because they're so accommodating and agreeable.
- Avoid conflict and confrontation as long as no deeply held value is threatened.

Leisure

Don't hurry, don't worry. You're only here for a short visit.
So be sure to stop and smell the flowers.
—WALTER HAGEN

ISFPs prefer part-time work so they have time to pursue the things they really care about, including being with family and friends. Many enjoy activities using their hands, such as painting, needlework, drawing, constructing, cooking, and home repair. They take pleasure in making their environment aesthetically pleasing. They are curious, love to explore the world around them, and enjoy nature. ISFPs have a respect for all living things.

Jogging is very beneficial. It's good for your legs and your feet.
It's also very good for the ground. It makes it feel needed.
—SNOOPY (CHARLES SCHULTZ)

Suggestions for ISFPs

- Become more assertive about things that are important to you.
- Express your opinions and feelings. Avoid "I don't know" or "Whatever you want" answers.
- If you are unfulfilled in your work, find a job that

expresses your ideals. Ask for help sorting out career options and priorities and then take action.

- Express your affection in words some of the time.
- Develop objectivity and a healthy skepticism toward people in order to recognize those who don't have your best interests at heart.
- Become aware of when you use activities as diversions to escape from pain and conflict.
- Avoid the tendency to leave projects unfinished and goals unmet when there are too many demands on you. Remember your own priorities and go after them.
- Break jobs down into manageable pieces. Use your short-term planning skills to get things done and acknowledge yourself when you meet each goal.
- Pay more attention to time, especially when being prompt affects those you care about.
- Be as gentle with yourself as you are with others. Beware of self-critical thoughts.

- Appreciate and value your accomplishments and all you give to others. The world needs your gifts.
- Appreciate your strengths—being adaptable, gentle, considerate, loyal, cooperative, understanding, spontaneous, and sensitive to others.

The highest form of wisdom is kindness.
—THE TALMUD

Chapter 11

Knowledge Seekers: The NT Temperament and the Four NT Types: ENTJ ENTP INTJ INTP

N: focuses on visions and possibilities.
T: decides according to objective, logical principles.

NTs at their best are innovative, inquisitive, analytical, bright, independent, witty, and competent.
NTs at their worst are arrogant, cynical, critical, distant, and self-righteous.

NTs value knowledge and competency. They prize intelligence in themselves and others, and feel compelled to constantly improve their base of knowledge. Problem-solving and mastering new challenges are stimulating. They are often ingenious and insightful, adept at theorizing and conceptualizing, and strive to understand and explain the world around them.

> *The more we know, the more we want to know: when we know enough,*
> *we know how much we don't know.*
> —CAROL ORLOCK

NTs understand and synthesize complex information, anticipate future trends, and focus on long-range goals. They enjoy new ways of doing things: developing, designing, and building models, theories, and systems. Dealing with day-to-day details and facts holds little or no interest to them, and is best if left to others. NTs aim for self-mastery in everything they do and want to make a unique contribution in their field of work.

NTs value independence and autonomy and dislike hierarchy and bureaucratic structure. They can be argumentative and opinionated when information from authorities contradicts what they believe. They prefer a work environment that is based on objective and fair standards, and where achieving major goals and breakthroughs is part of the routine.

NTs desire recognition and admiration mainly from peers who are competent in their field. They have strong convictions, trust their own judgments, and stand on principles no matter what the consequences. They are skeptical of public opinion.

NTs can come across as know-it-alls and be critical of others' ideas. They are complex and can be difficult for people of other temperaments to understand. Because of the high standards they set for themselves, they can have a sense of inadequacy and self-doubt about their capabilities. Sometimes they become self-critical, disheartened, and/or depressed if their own need for self-improvement falls short of these standards.

NTs share connections of the mind more than those of the heart. They like relating through mental challenges such as interesting discussions, or games of chess and bridge. They enjoy intellectual exchanges and like to argue and debate many sides of an issue.

NTs often live for their work and intellectual pursuits. Relationships can take a backseat. NTs can be oblivious of social conventions and may forget to observe rituals such as anniversaries or birthdays. They are more comfortable expressing thoughts than feelings, and can be unaware and uncomfortable with others' feelings and sensitivities. They dislike discussing personal issues and sentimentality, but they can let their guard down with people they trust. If they feel rejected, they usually keep it to themselves.

NT parents place strong value on knowledge and learning. They foster intellectual independence and want their children to grow up expressing independent thought. They take family responsibilities seriously but can pursue their careers and intellectual interests at the expense of spending time with their families. Expressing warmth and affection to their children can be difficult. NTs with a preference for Judging (ENTJ, INTJ) are often firm and consistent disciplinarians and tend to be controlling. NTs with a preference for Perceiving (ENTP, INTP) are often more accepting and tolerant of their children's differences and don't try to impose their will on them.

NT children and teens enjoy learning but need to be challenged or they may become bored. They are inquisitive and constantly questioning.

NTs can be argumentative, strong-willed, and opinionated, and they are sensitive to being treated unjustly or unfairly. They are frequently either high achievers, at the top of their class (more often ENTJ or INTJ), or they feel school is a waste of time and are not interested in grades (more often ENTP or INTP). They like to be independent and often study subjects unrelated to the curriculum.

> *I have never let my schooling interfere with my education.*
> —MARK TWAIN

College is often more challenging and rewarding where they have more independence and can find other NTs to relate to. NTs with a preference for Extraverting (ENTJ, ENTP) are often sociable and involved in school activities. NTs with a preference for Introverting (INTJ, INTP) enjoy being alone with their interests and are not as likely to participate in social activities.

How to get along with NTs

- Let them know you appreciate their objectivity, knowledge, quick minds, and wit.
- Respect their need for independence and autonomy.
- Develop your own interests. Don't rely on them for all your companionship. Avoid being smothering or overly dependent.
- Engage in interesting and intellectually stimulating conversation with them.
- When communicating, try not to overwhelm them with your feelings.
- Don't be afraid to debate with them, and if you do, don't take their remarks personally.
- If you value the wisdom of their counsel and advice, make sure you let them know—frequently!

Tips for NTs

Be wiser than other people if you can, but do not tell them so.
—LORD CHESTERFIELD

- Make time for your relationships. Avoid taking your loved ones for granted.

- Learn to listen and avoid analyzing or being critical when others are telling you their problems. Many times, people just want understanding and to be heard; not every problem needs to be solved.
- Avoid talking over other peoples' heads. Try to use vocabulary that is appropriate for the situation and company.
- Learn to express your emotional side and practice sharing your softness with people you trust.
- Pay attention to the practical applications of your ideas rather than just the innovative implications.

Idealism is fine; but as it approaches reality, the cost becomes prohibitive.
—WILLIAM F. BUCKLEY, JR.

- Develop your Sensing side by enjoying good food, exercise, sensuality, or simply the joy of a flower in a garden.

- Notice the effect your behavior has on others. Be aware of people reacting defensively or withdrawing, as if they are intimidated by you.
- Learn to access your heart and body as well as your mind for information. Pay attention to physical clues in your body to help you identify your emotions and feelings.
- Recognize the limits of rational thinking and cerebral understanding.

- Do things just for the fun of it, not just to become more competent or to have more control.

Now that you have an understanding of the NT temperament, it will be easier to learn about the four NT Types.

ENTJ
Extraverting   INtuiting   Thinking   Judging

E: is energized by the outer world.
N: focuses on visions and possibilities.
T: decides according to objective, logical principles.
J: wants things settled and decided.

ENTJs are dynamic, energetic, confident, and competent. They naturally move into positions where they can take charge and mobilize resources to achieve long-range goals. They are knowledgeable, they enjoy confrontation, and they like to engage in intellectually stimulating exchanges. ENTJs like and respect people who challenge them and have little or no respect for those who don't.

> *I love an opposition that has convictions.*
> —FREDERICK THE GREAT

ENTJs at Work

- Like to be in charge; are often in authority positions as executives, administrators, and leaders.

> *Power is the ultimate aphrodisiac.*
> —HENRY KISSINGER

- Are change-oriented leaders who like to set the goals and provide overall direction, leaving the detailed execution to subordinates.
- See obstacles as challenges; stay focused on resolving problems, reaching conclusions, and moving ahead.

- Look for the most strategic ways to accomplish their goals.
- Organize their facts and strategies in advance and like to get things done ahead of schedule.
- Dislike inefficiency, incompetence, and indecisiveness; are tough on people if they fall short of their expectations.
- Are competitive and driven; often workaholics.
- Prefer to work with strong-minded, independent, results-oriented people.
- Are not likely to be convinced by anything but good, solid reasoning.
- Like to be in charge of decision-making; dislike taking instructions or advice from others unless that person is seen as having greater knowledge or competence.
- Provide logical approaches to problems and like to work within a clear and definite set of guidelines.

Typical Occupations

Many different careers are suitable for ENTJs. The following is a list of some occupations that have proven to be satisfying for many ENTJs.

administrator	labor relations worker
bank manager	lawyer
business manager	manager
computer specialist	marketer
consultant	physician
corporate team trainer	psychologist
curriculum designer	research and development specialist
economist	researcher
engineer	scientist
environmental planner	stockbroker
financial planner	systems analyst
health and education consultant	

ENTJs in Relationships

- Are honest, direct, and straightforward. They have strong convictions and don't hesitate to express them.
- Encourage people they care about to improve themselves in ways which they are convinced are in their best interest.
- Live life with gusto and enthusiasm.
- Have a gregarious, fun-loving side as well as a serious and driven side.
- Want relationships to be an opportunity for learning.
- Value prestige and status; some like being with a partner who helps their image of success.
- Need a mate who is autonomous and has good self-esteem.
- Can be impatient when things are not done according to their plans.
- Can be intimidating, blunt, and abrasive.
- Can hide their soft, sentimental side with a show of toughness.
- Can have explosive outbursts or judgments on themselves and others when stressed.

Leisure

A perpetual holiday is a good working definition of hell.
—GEORGE BERNARD SHAW

ENTJs have an improvement plan for everything, including leisure. As with all aspects of their life, leisure has to have a purpose. They enjoy the kind of social events that allow them to engage in mentally stimulating exchanges. Some like to mix business with pleasure, such as playing handball with clients. When things get dull or when they're not in charge, ENTJs can become impatient and bored.

WALTER'S COMPANY SENT HIM AWAY ON A STRESS REDUCTION RETREAT.

Suggestions for ENTJs

- Avoid driving others as hard as you drive yourself. Discover how much is "good enough" and learn to recognize when you need to let things be.
- Schedule time every day for rest and relaxation. Practice meditation or stress reduction techniques.

The time you enjoy wasting is not wasted time.
—BERTRAND RUSSELL

- Try to anticipate your loved ones' most important needs and ask others what you can do for them.
- Leave your need to control on the doorstep when you come home to your family.

- Beware of misinterpreting criticism as an attempt to control you. Be especially careful when you think someone is challenging your competency. Find out what the person means before reacting.
- Be aware of your effect on others. Avoid appearing overly confident or aggressive and control your temper. Remember that what you see as hearty exchanges and debates may not be perceived that way by others.
- Consider the commonsense advice and input of others instead of charging ahead on your own. Take time to reflect, to discover new insights or information, and to look at things from different perspectives before making decisions.

- Enjoy the moment for what it is, not for what you can make of it or how you can structure it.
- Remember that everyone is here with different gifts to give. Learn to offer encouragement and to validate and appreciate other people's contributions.
- Learn to compromise and to give in once in a while. Work at negotiating solutions that provide some of what everyone needs.
- Appreciate your strengths—being resourceful, organized, efficient, objective, assertive, inquisitive, confident, innovative, and having leadership and planning skills.

ENTP
Extraverting   INtuiting   Thinking   Perceiving

E: is energized by the external world.
N: focuses on visions and possibilities.
T: decides according to objective, logical principles.
P: wants things left open and flexible.

ENTPs are energetic, enthusiastic, gregarious, and confident. Many are nonconformists and like to work or outwit the system. They are innovative and ingenious in inventing new ways of doing things. ENTPs have excellent analytical ability and are resourceful in solving challenging problems, especially theoretical ones. They like variety and change, and are resistant to anything that limits, traps, or bores them.

> *Consistency is contrary to nature, contrary to life.*
> *The only completely consistent people are the dead.*
> —ALDOUS HUXLEY

ENTPs at Work

- Use ingenuity to solve problems; they trust their ability to improvise and think on their feet.
- Are clever and imaginative in dealing with others and are good at convincing others of their point of view.
- Like to follow their own time frame and ignore traditional ways of doing things.
- Can be inspirational and rise to leadership positions because of their quick minds, confidence, and verbal skill.
- Prefer the start-up to the maintenance phase of a project; divising new projects is more exciting than following through with routine tasks to complete the project.

A good idea will keep you awake during the morning, but a great idea
will keep you awake during the night.
—MARILYN VOS SAVANT

- Like to juggle many things at once and will become bored quickly if their job does not allow for variety and innovation.
- Work best with a succession of stimulating projects, especially when interacting with many different people.
- Have difficulty narrowing their focus because so many things are interesting to them.

Typical Occupations

Many different careers are suitable for ENTPs. The following is a list of some occupations that have proven to be satisfying for many ENTPs.

actor	mortgage broker
advertising director	physician
attorney	psychologist
computer analyst	public relations worker
consultant	public speaker
corporate team trainer	real-estate developer
engineer	research and development specialist
entrepreneur	salesperson
financial planner	social scientist
inventor	university professor
marketer	writer

ENTPs in Relationships

- Are optimistic, charming, quick-witted, and make good conversationalists.
- Value their freedom and independence.
- Prefer to understand people rather than judge them and pay attention to the underlying motivations of others.
- Are constantly thinking of new things to try; can be ready to go as soon as a new idea is suggested.
- Like being with a partner who is mentally stimulating and enjoys new experiences and adventures.
- Seek growth, excitement, and continuous improvement in their relationships.
- Can be arrogant, argumentative, and insensitive.
- Enjoy debating; can take any side of an argument, and like to have the last word.

Too much agreement kills a chat.
—ELDRIDGE CLEAVER

- Go back and forth between enthusiastic participation and being self-absorbed and preoccupied with their own ideas.
- May deny emotional pain and keep busy to avoid dealing with their feelings.
- Can be distant and keep relationships on a superficial level.

Leisure

Given all their interests, schemes, and adventures, life can feel too short for ENTPs. Relaxation comes from seeking new outlets and doing new things. They enjoy the limelight, laughter, and sharing their ideas and activities with friends. Their home is likely to be open to everyone, and they enjoy traveling to exotic places and attending unusual events. They prefer to stay open to whatever seems most fun rather than plan their leisure time.

Suggestions for ENTPs

- Avoid squandering your energies on too many projects. Try to pick those that have the most potential value and focus on them.
- Estimate the time you think a project will take, and whatever that is, double it.
- Try to ally yourself with someone who enjoys the follow-through phase of a project.

- When presenting an idea, prepare in advance rather than just relying on improvisation. This can help you gain more support for your projects.

> *The best impromptu speeches are the ones written well in advance.*
> —RUTH GORDON

- Remember that your endless ideas can be tiring to others. Keep some of them to yourself.

- Learn to work within the system or arrange things to become self-employed so you can thrive on the autonomy you crave.
- Avoid overextending yourself, partying too much, or overindulging to the point of saturation. Make time for activities that can help release stress and excess energy wisely.

> *Half an hour's meditation is essential except when you are very busy.*
> *Then a full hour is needed.*
> —FRANCIS DE SALES

- Remember that arguing, debating, and matching wits can be fun for some people, but it will wear others out.
- Avoid interrupting others and learn the benefits of listening.
- Be accountable. Take deadlines seriously. Respect others' time and need for planning.

- Slow down and pay attention to the simple facts and joys of everyday life all around you. Create times when there's nothing you have to do.

There is more to life than increasing its speed.
—Mahatma Gandhi

- Learn to accept your emotional pain and negative feelings. They are natural parts of life.
- Appreciate your strengths—being ingenious, enthusiastic, competent, adaptable, innovative, resourceful, conceptual, and curious.

INTJ
Introverting   INtuiting   Thinking   Judging

I: is energized by their internal world.

N: focuses on visions and possibilities.

T: decides according to objective, logical principles.

J: wants things settled and decided.

INTJs have a mental model of how things ought to be and constantly seek to improve themselves, others, and everything around them. They are innovators in the field of ideas, and are confident of their visions and inspirations regardless of popular beliefs and others' skepticism. INTJs have a strong need for autonomy and are highly independent. They prefer to do things their way.

As one goes through life one learns that if you don't paddle your own canoe,
you don't move.
—Katharine Hepburn

INTJs at Work

- Have strong conceptual strengths; can be brilliant and original and are often visionaries.
- Have great confidence in their intuitive insights and are intent on turning them into reality.

Winning the prize wasn't half as exciting as doing the work itself.
—Maria Mayer (1963 Nobel Prize in Physics)

- Often rise to leadership or executive positions offering a new sense of purpose, vision, or mission for an organization.
- Work in a logical and orderly way to develop innovative solutions to problems.
- Build systems, develop strategies, and apply theoretical models that are right for the challenge at hand.
- Can be obsessed with a goal; drive others as hard as they drive themselves.

- Can become self-critical and frustrated when reality doesn't meet their model of perfection.

One never notices what has been done; one can only see what remains to be done.
—MARIE CURIE

- Like to work independently, without interruption.
- Want to maintain control over the execution of their ideas.

Typical Occupations

Many different careers are suitable for INTJs. The following is a list of some occupations that have proven to be satisfying for many INTJs.

administrator	mathematician
archaeologist	mortgage broker
architect	photographer
astonomer	physician
attorney	psychiatrist
computer programmer or analyst	psychologist
consultant	researcher
designer	scientist
economist	social scientist
engineer	stockbroker
inventor	university professor
investment or business analyst	writer
management consultant	

INTJs in Relationships

- Are reserved and aloof.

Santa Claus has the right idea: visit people once a year.
—VICTOR BORGE

- Are very loyal and are usually drawn to traditional relationships.
- Show their affections only with those close to them.
- Like low-key, intimate, one-on-one social time.

- Are often attracted to outgoing types who help lighten them up and get them out of their seriousness.
- Are intellectually engaging and enjoy an exchange of ideas.
- Dislike small talk; don't want to waste their time socializing unless they can learn something in the process.

I prefer tongue-tied knowledge to ignorant loquacity.
—CICERO

- Can be frugal with their time and resources unless it fits with what is important and of value to them.

- Are sensitive to rejection but hide their hurt from others and tend to keep their vulnerability to themselves.
- Are absorbed in their work and can neglect being attentive in their relationships.
- Can be stubborn about their own point of view, believing they have the absolute truth, and can be unaware of how their behavior affects others.

Leisure

INTJs like quiet, uninterrupted alone time for reflecting, reading, dreaming, and studying new subjects. Many like keeping their body in shape so their minds will work better. They like individual sports such as running, swimming, and backpacking. INTJs are disciplined and their free time is scheduled and purposeful. They enjoy activities where they can learn something in the process, such as attending films, cultural events, informational lectures, and visiting museums. Mastery in anything they undertake is important.

Suggestions for INTJs

- Solicit input from others and be open to having your ideas challenged.
- Avoid being self-righteous and defensive. Don't reject others' views outright just because they are different from yours.
- Pay attention to physical symptoms of stress before they get to the crisis stage. Recognize your limitations and slow down your pace.
- Show appreciation to others based on merit, not just on your standards of perfection. Don't demand of others the same intensity you demand of yourself.
- If you want to improve your relationships with others, beware of being aloof, demanding, or insensitive with criticism.
- In a negative situation, be willing to take responsibility for your part.
- Learn to be flexible. Be willing to give in on less important points and details with others.

- Consider working for yourself. Many INTJs are too independent to work for others or in the corporate world and are good at creating something new.
- Make time for artistic pursuits or creative hobbies that have no immediate purpose or application.
- Let go of trying to control everything in life.

- Appreciate your strengths—being innovative, organized, ingenious, determined, self-confident, independent, and able to grasp the complex.

INTP
Introverting   INtuiting   Thinking   Perceiving

I: is energized by their internal world.

N: focuses on visions and possibilities.

T: decides according to objective, logical principles.

P: wants things left open and flexible.

INTPs are quiet, reserved, self-reliant, and highly independent. They are introspective and constantly in search of inner consistency. Being precise, concise, and articulate is important. They have a rich inner world of thoughts and ideas with a driving curiosity to understand the universe and to examine its universal truths and principles.

> *The eternal mystery of the world is its incomprehensibility.*
> —ALBERT EINSTEIN

INTPs at Work

- Are good at developing complex systems and conceptual models but like to leave application and implementation to others.
- Have high standards of intellectual and professional competence and pride themselves on self-mastery.
- Seek logical purity of thought and strive to be ingenious in their conceptualizations.
- Examine all options carefully and arrive at definite, well-supported conclusions.
- Can have difficulty articulating their deep insights so that others can understand.

> *Syzgy, inexorable, pancreative, phantasmagoria—anyone who can use those four words in one sentence will never have to do manual labor.*
> —W. P. KINSELLA

- Notice inconsistencies, contradictions, and logical flaws in their own and others' thinking.
- Can get carried away with conceptualizing and reduce everything to a set of classification schemes.

- Persevere until they comprehend an issue in all its complexity; they move on once something is thoroughly understood.
- Like to set their own goals and standards in a flexible, unstructured environment.
- Can become cynical or depressed if they can't find outlets for their innovative abilities.
- Like working independently, but can have difficulty following things through to completion.
- Dislike supervising others, or mediating interpersonal differences.

Typical Occupations

Many different careers that are suitable for INTPs. The following is a list of some occupations that have proven to be satisfying for many INTPs.

archaeologist	inventor
architect	mathematician
artist	musician
astronomer	philosopher
attorney	photographer
biologist	physician
chemist	psychiatrist
computer analyst or programmer	psychologist
engineer	researcher
financial planner	scientist
graphic designer	university professor
historian	writer

AN INTP'S WORST JOB

INTPs in Relationships

- Are absorbed in their thoughts, interests, and work and can neglect their relationships.
- Are loyal to those who are important to them and show their feelings in subtle ways.
- Can easily feel intruded upon and drained from too much contact with others.
- Like a calm, conflict-free atmosphere.
- Are not very concerned with physical appearance or what others think of them.
- Dislike commercialism and don't look to material possessions for happiness.

Wealth consists not in having outer possessions, but in having inner treasures.
—SUFI WISDOM

- Have a dry wit and rich sense of humor.
- Can be formal and distant with strangers and acquaintances, but are generally open-minded and accepting of people as they get to know them.
- Dislike small talk but love to discuss and debate conceptual things.
- Can be arrogant and intellectually snobbish.

- Are often attracted to outgoing partners who provide a bridge to the outside world.

Leisure

I have always imagined that Paradise will be a kind of library.
—Jorge Luis Borges

INTPs enjoy engaging in many activities alone. They tend to have interests and hobbies that absorb their attention to the exclusion of other people. Some INTPs enjoy physical challenges and many like games of mental strategy such as bridge, chess, and wordplays. INTPs are lifelong learners and are always improving and expanding their intellect.

EMMA WAS BUSY GETTING HER FIFTEENTH COLLEGE DEGREE.

Suggestions for INTPs

- Be sensitive to others' desires and needs. Learn about what matters personally to those you care about.
- Beware of being overly critical, condescending, or so focused on what you are saying that you ignore others' lack of interest.
- Learn to simplify what you write or say so that others will be able to understand you.
- Express appreciation and acknowledgment for others' accomplishments and talents. Give praise even for the little things.
- Don't put off making decisions just because there is one flaw in your plan. Move plans out of the conceptual stage and take action.

At the day of judgment, we shall not be asked what we have read
but what we have done.
—Thomas à Kempis

- Learn to be more self-revealing and experiment with communicating how you feel inside.
- Speak up in group discussions even though a thought or idea may seem obvious to you.
- Avoid responding defensively when your logic or ideas are challenged.
- Beware of being so busy observing and figuring out life that you may forget to participate in life itself.
- Appreciate your strengths—being innovative, principled, logical, independent, ingenious, scholarly, analytical, theoretical, and precise in thought and language.

Chapter 12

Ideal Seekers: The NF Temperament and the Four NF Types:
ENFJ ENFP INFJ INFP

N: focuses on visions and possibilities.
F: decides according to personal values.

NFs at their best are compassionate, warm, loyal, helpful, idealistic, and genuine.

NFs at their worst are hypersensitive, overly emotional, judgmental, impractical, unrealistic, and self-absorbed.

NFs direct their iNtuition and insight toward understanding themselves and others. They value integrity and strive for genuineness and authenticity.

NFs tend to have a vision of an ideal world and want to work toward creating that vision here on earth. Seen as overly optimistic by others, they genuinely strive for an ideal they believe is real. They enjoy work that allows them to use their creativity and individuality, and are not content to just make a living. NFs like to use their insight to benefit other people and many focus their attention and energy on helping others to realize their potential. They are often sensitive to others' emotional needs and are skillful at bringing out the best in people. They can be disappointed when projects or people don't turn out as they expected, because they put so much faith and energy into them.

They like working in a friendly, conflict-free environment where personal and professional growth and development are encouraged. They can be self-righteous about their values and take offense if others don't accept their ideas. Working with people who don't encourage, appreciate, and affirm them can be difficult. They have a strong desire for harmony and are good at conflict resolution.

NFs like being mentally stimulated and coming up with new ideas and solutions. After the initial challenge or newness disappears, they can get bored with a project. They dislike standard procedures and tight supervision and can be too idealistic and independent-minded to work in most corporate, government, or military environments. NFs can have an anti-authoritarian attitude and often take sides with the underdog.

NFs are warmhearted, affirming, nurturing, and empathic. They can become overly involved in other people's psyches and lives, and must guard against sympathizing with another's hurt beyond what the person is actually experiencing. They dream of having a deeply fulfilling and meaningful relationship with an "ideal" partner. They like talking with their partner about plans and goals for the future. Many NFs enjoy shar-

ing ideas, values, dreams, philosophy, spirituality, and new ways of seeing things. A lot of effort, emotion, and enthusiasm is invested in their relationships, sometimes more than a partner of another temperament is comfortable with. They frequently respond to the emotional demands of others and can feel overwhelmed, pressured, and exhausted if they don't set boundaries. If they feel too suffocated by others, they can disappear.

NFs seek self-actualization and meaning in their lives, and are interested in understanding and expressing their feelings. They can become self-absorbed in their search for identity, tending to take everything personally. They are easily hurt, sometimes even crushed, by criticism.

As parents, NFs are affirming and encouraging and feel a strong sense of responsibility to help develop their children's minds and spirits. They try to motivate, mold, and direct their children toward worthwhile goals and values. They can be good listeners and tolerant of a child's moods and emotions. NFs encourage their children's individuality and creativity even if very different from their own.

NFs who have a Perceiving preference (ENFP, INFP) often have a relaxed parenting style and can find it hard to set boundaries and to provide structure and consistency. NFs who have a Judging preference (ENFJ, INFJ) tend to be more consistent, systematic, and predictable as parents. Their boundaries are more clearly defined.

As children and teens, NFs have rich and active imaginations. They are curious and innovative and are often involved in creative activities. They are satisfied with the broad grasp of a subject without needing to master the facts or details. They are cooperative and want to be affirmed by adults and other children. They can, however, be unyielding if they feel misunderstood or if their values are violated. Tense or hostile environments are especially difficult for children of this temperament.

NFs with a preference for Extraverting (ENFJ, ENFP) tend to be outgoing, talkative, and gregarious. NFs with a preference for Introverting (INFJ, INFP) are more reserved and absorbed with their inner world.

How to get along with NFs

Brevity may be the soul of wit, but not when someone's saying, "I love you."
—JUDITH VIORST

- They enjoy romance and attention, so give them cards, gifts, compliments, hugs, adoration, and other forms of loving attention.
- Appreciate them for the deep love they are capable of giving and expressing.

- Reassure them that if they say no, you will not reject them or be angry with them.
- Be tactful when offering feedback. NFs are sensitive to disapproval, rejection, sarcasm, and teasing. Criticism of their unique ways can damage their self-esteem.
- Encourage them to follow their personal and creative pursuits, and to put their work out in the world.
- Be understanding and patient about their need to process and express their feelings.
- Don't judge them for their changing moods.

Tips for NFs

- Look for work that fits your ideals and interests. Make sure it allows you to be an individual and express yourself.
- Avoid taking every comment and remark personally.
- Remember that people are human and that a mix of good and bad qualities in everyone is natural. Don't let your expectations be too unrealistic.
- Be aware of blaming others or finding fault with them when they don't meet your expectations.
- Avoid becoming overly involved in other people's lives. Keep a balanced focus between their needs and yours.

To love oneself is the beginning of a lifelong romance.
—Oscar Wilde

- Notice your tendency to project ideal qualities onto others. When meeting someone new, engage in reality testing and ask practical questions before leaping into a relationship.

- Avoid being overly solicitous and overly giving. Learn to say no.
- Beware of encouraging others' dependence on you.
- Become more in touch with your senses. Learn to be connected with your body and with nature.
- Learn to enjoy the present and the everyday realities of life. Accept the gifts of each moment.
- Learn to be more objective and to impersonally examine the consequences of your choices and action.
- Discern what is actually being communicated, not just what is between the lines.

> *Rose-colored glasses are never made in bifocals.*
> *Nobody wants to read the small print in dreams.*
> —ANN LANDERS

- Find friends who understand and appreciate you. Go to places where other NFs are likely to be, such as classes in psychology, literature, art, or spirituality.
- Set realistic goals so you don't feel frustrated and disappointed when you don't accomplish all you hoped to. Wallowing in guilt and self-reproach is a waste of time.
- Value your unique contributions and strive to be your authentic self.

Now that you have an understanding of the NF temperament, it will be easier to learn about the four NF types.

ENFJ
Extraverting   INtuiting   Feeling   Judging

E: is energized by the external world.

N: focuses on visions and possibilities.

F: decides according to personal values.

J: wants things settled and decided.

ENFJs are caring and concerned and they focus on people's most admirable qualities. They have exuberant, charming, and enthusiastic personalities and get along well with lots of different people. ENFJs are excellent communicators, natural leaders, and are good at motivating and persuading others.

ENFJs at Work

> *You really* can *change the world if you care enough.*
> —MARION WRIGHT EDELMAN

- Are ambitious and willing to work hard to achieve and materialize their ideals.
- Are conscientious, orderly, goal-oriented, and decisive; expect the same of others.
- Express themselves well and have a smooth, easy way with words.
- Are good at knowing what a group needs to reach its goals and at initiating the action to make it happen.
- Respect a variety of opinions and are good at creating team spirit.
- Like working with creative and energetic people in an active, challenging environment with a variety of activities.
- Will follow policies and procedures as long as they are compatible with the values and needs of the people they affect.
- When faced with setbacks, can accept them as a new challenge.
- Prefer occupations that reflect their ideals and allow them to bring inspiration and harmony to others.
- Tend to take quick action and are often in a hurry; can be impatient and frustrated with slow processes.
- Like having control and being responsible for their own projects.

Typical Occupations

Many different careers are suitable for ENFJs. The following is a list of some occupations that have proven satisfying for many ENFJs.

actor

administrator

advertising

clergy

corporate or team trainer

designer

dietician or nutritionist

fund-raiser

holistic health practitioner

motivational speaker

organizational development consultant

performer

physical therapist

psychologist or therapist

public relations specialist

recruiter

religious educator

resource development specialist

sales representative

social worker

speech pathologist

teacher or professor

vocational counselor

writer or editor

ENFJs in Relationships

I have a fear of being disliked, even by people I dislike.
—OPRAH WINFREY

- Are friendly, warm, and genuinely like to please people.
- Try hard to promote harmonious, affirming, cooperative relationships.
- Are loyal and devoted friends.
- Can idealize their partner and overlook incompatabilities.
- Try to emulate the best qualities of those they admire.
- Like to be reassured of their value by receiving praise, respect, and affirmation.

I can live for two months on a good compliment.
—MARK TWAIN

- Dislike giving or getting negative feedback, but can be confrontive when necessary.
- Can become depressed if their sincerity is questioned.

- Have many shoulds and should nots.
- Can have difficulty getting in touch with their inner world of feelings.
- Often feel responsible for other people's feelings and find it difficult to detach or set boundaries.
- Are conflicted between their need for personal achievement versus the need to please and support others.

Leisure

ENFJs have a broad range of interests and like to have an active lifestyle. They need to be with people and can become moody or bored if they have too much time alone. Their leisure is scheduled and planned, and responsibilities are put before play. They enjoy reading, discussing ideas, organizing events, and participating in community organizations and humanitarian causes.

Suggestions for ENFJs

- Stop trying to do it all. Some things can wait and others don't need to happen at all.
- Try to reduce stress by appreciating and acknowledging your present level of success and achievement.

- Learn to relax.
- Pay attention to which activities and projects are most satisfying to you, and then try to focus on those.
- Beware of idealizing people and being overly loyal.
- Try to be less dependent on external affirmation and learn what *you* value instead of what others value.

- Learn to face conflicts. Although you have a strong need for harmony, don't avoid dealing with difficulty.
- Look out for excessive responsiveness to other people's needs and demands. Realize that you can't be everything to everyone.

NO, I REALLY CAN'T TALK RIGHT NOW. I'M IN THE MIDDLE OF SOMETHING.

- Learn to ask for the same support that you give to others.
- Be watchful of your tendency for smooth talk and flattery. It can sound phony and be smothering if overdone or misunderstood.
- Learn to take advice, not just give it.
- Avoid coming to decisions prematurely. Consider more than one option before acting.

ADVICE TAKEN
I'LL PAY 10¢

- Become aware of the difference between your real feelings and the feelings you put on because they seem more appropriate.
- Appreciate your strengths of compassion, enthusiasm, warmth, sensitivity, optimism, empathy, leadership, and insightfulness.

ENFP
Extraverting INtuiting Feeling Perceiving

E: is energized by the external world.
N: focuses on visions and possibilities.
F: decides according to personal values.
P: wants things left open and flexible.

ENFPs are outgoing, dynamic, lively, and spontaneous. They often have a good sense of humor and their enthusiasm and joy for life can be contagious. ENFPs have rich imaginations and active minds. Their thoughts are always wandering and their moods ever changing. They can be on one track in one minute and on another track in the next.

Consistency is the last refuge of the unimaginative.
—OSCAR WILDE

ENFPs at Work

- Dislike handling factual details, including financial matters.

Life is too short to balance a checkbook.
—HOWARD OGDEN

- Seek variety and challenge, constantly searching for new outlets and imaginative ways of doing things.
- Can be inspiring and charismatic leaders; they motivate others with their energy and enthusiasm.
- Like to work collaboratively in stimulating environments with creative and energetic people.
- Are enthusiastic about initiating projects but can lose interest once they're started. Starting is more fun than finishing.
- Can lose all sense of time and their physical needs when caught up in their projects. Often forget to eat or sleep when fully engaged.
- Are good at improvising and thinking on their feet.
- Are often talented in many areas, but can have difficulty narrowing their focus.

- Can become overwhelmed by details and paralyzed by their lack of organization; want someone else to take over the routine and follow-up.

> *I love being a writer. What I can't stand is the paperwork.*
> —Peter De Vries

- Want to work at their own pace with a minimum of structure or supervision.

Typical Occupations

Many different careers are suitable for ENFPs. The following is a list of some occupations that have proven to be satisfying for many ENFPs.

actor	journalist
advertising director	marketer
artist	media specialist
clergy	mediator
conference planner	motivational speaker
consultant	psychotherapist
corporate or team trainer	public relations worker
entertainer	recruiter
entrepreneur	religious educator
food and personal services	sales
holistic health practitioner	small business owner
human resource development specialist	teacher
interior decorator	writer

ENFPs in Relationships

- Can make closeness and intimacy a full-time pursuit.
- Are keenly perceptive about what is going on with people.
- Know how to establish instant rapport and make people feel comfortable.
- Focus their attention intensely on another person; can make others feel unconditionally loved.
- Idealize and romanticize their current partner, project, or event. They're always involved or in love, with someone or something new.

- Value their freedom and autonomy.
- Like emotional intensity and enjoy expressing a wide range of feelings.
- Want to be special; seek approval and affirmation from those important to them.
- Can be charming and flirtatious.
- Relate with warmth and affection to many people.

- Can appear overly enthusiastic, positive, and optimistic and are sometimes seen as insincere.

Leisure

ENFPs enjoy telling stories, being center stage, and having meaningful conversations. They often like attending workshops and classes and belonging to many groups. Quieter activities such as reading, writing, and creative projects are also pleasurable, but they don't like to do them alone for too long. They have a knack for making ordinary events exciting and fun, without much planning. ENFPs enjoy keeping their life active, spontaneous, and pursuing new experiences.

Suggestions for ENFPs

- Avoid squandering your energy by going in too many directions. Be clear about what you want to devote your time and energy to.
- Know and accept your limitations. Avoid the tendency of overcommitting yourself and then feeling stressed and fragmented.
- Once you decide on a course of action don't give up on it for some new idea or option that comes along. Persevere through the duller routines of life.
- Don't let impromptu socializing or other distractions take you away from less exciting but nonetheless important tasks.

- Make commitments that are realistic.
- Practice breaking large projects into component parts and take all the necessary steps to make them happen.
- When starting a project, pay attention to what will actually be required. Factor in the details and facts in order to estimate how long an activity will take. Leave extra time, "just in case."
- Consider working for yourself since you can be individualistic and rebellious.
- Avoid rushing into new relationships. Take your time getting to know people.
- Consider how others will be affected by what you say before you blurt out your feelings.
- Avoid offering "helpful" insights when not asked. Check to see if others want your advice and opinions.

- Take your time settling down. Wait until you're older to make final relationship and career choices.

- Appreciate your strengths of creativity, optimism, individualism, enthusiasm, spontaneity, perceptiveness, curiosity, expressiveness, friendliness, and adapt-ability.

INFJ
Introverting   INtuiting   Feeling   Judging

I: is energized by their internal world.
N: focuses on visions and possibilities.
F: decides according to personal values.
J: wants things settled and decided.

INFJs have a quiet, low-key presence and are compassionate, concerned, and tender-hearted. Their complex personalities are often puzzling to others, even to themselves. They have a rich imagination and inner life and are keenly aware of the emotions and motivations of others. They are committed to their inspirations and ideals and inspire insight and growth in others.

INFJs at Work

- Are highly creative and original; often great visionaries.
- Work toward long-range goals and follow through on their commitments; want to see their ideas developed and applied.
- Can be highly demanding of themselves and others; value self-improvement and are often perfectionists.
- Are single-minded and determined when defending their values and beliefs.
- Pursue their ideals and goals quietly and diligently.
- Often make significant contributions to the welfare of humankind.
- See setbacks as problems to be solved rather than insurmountable obstacles.
- Are clear and eloquent in their use of words; often prefer writing over speaking.
- Think things through carefully, are good at concentrating, and dislike distractions.
- Prefer working in a quiet, organized setting that supports their inner concentration.
- Want admiration and respect but do not tend to call attention to themselves.
- Can be persuasive and inspirational leaders if they are willing to be visible.
- Want to organize their own time and have control over both the process and product.

Typical Occupations

Many different careers are suitable for INFJs. The following is a list of some occupations that have proven to be satisfying for many INFJs.

architect

artist

clergy

consultant

designer

dietician or nutritionist

editor

health care administrator

holistic health practitioner

interpreter or translator

librarian

media specialist

musician or composer

occupational therapist

philosopher

physician

program designer

psychotherapist

religious educator

researcher

scientist

social scientist

speech pathologist

teacher or professor

writer

INFJs in Relationships

- Are tender and gentle; others find it pleasant to be in their presence or company.
- Have a strong nesting instinct and desire to create a comfortable home.
- Are cautious about making a commitment, but when it is right, commitment fulfills their highest purpose and they give it their all.

- Are capable of deep intimacy and can lose themselves in favor of their lover's needs.
- Are good listeners and communicate articulately when they feel comfortable.
- Share their feelings, emotions, and affections in private, and only with a small number of close friends.

- Often feel responsible for other people's feelings and can find it hard to maintain healthy boundaries.
- Can be moody, melancholy, and obsessed with their intense inner world.
- Are very sensitive to criticism and rejection and feel deeply hurt when they are not understood.

It is a terrible thing
To be so open: it is as if my heart
Put on a face and walked into the world.
—Sylvia Plath, "A Poem for Three Voices"

- Can have difficulty voicing their thoughts and perceptions in words that others can understand.
- Can be lighthearted and playful when they feel relaxed.
- Have a strong need for harmony; can feel tense, frustrated, and even get ill when they are not able to attain it.
- Handle situations tactfully when it is necessary to confront someone.

Leisure

INFJs like a balance between time alone for their many creative projects, and time with friends and family at intimate gatherings. A comfortable, orderly, aesthetically pleasing home is important to them. Many INFJs enjoy attending artistic and cultural events. INFJs tend to spend more time with mental and emotional pursuits rather than physical ones and their rich inner life keeps them very busy.

Loneliness is the poverty of self; solitude is the richness of self.
—May Sarton

Suggestions for INFJs

- Respect your need for time alone to dream, fantasize, explore theories, read, and create.
- Share your ideas, visions, feelings, and inner richness with the people you are close to.
- Try to be direct in your communication. Don't silently withdraw as a way of setting limits; this can leave others feeling hurt and confused.

- Try to give affection when others need it, not only when you feel the inspiration.
- Be realistic about how much acceptance you can reasonably expect from others. Realize that rejection of your thoughts and ideas is not a rejection of you.
- Avoid overdosing on self-analysis. Express your feelings through writing, art, or talking. Then move on.

- See your moods as transitory. Know that they will change.

Hope is the feeling you have that the feeling you have isn't permanent.
—Jean Kerr

- Avoid wasting time over mundane details and routines just to be organized. Decide what is important and what to set aside.
- Refrain from trying to order and control life. Let the universe do its thing.

No snowflake ever falls in the wrong place.
—Zen saying

- Slow down the pace of life. Be aware of overextending yourself.
- Try to embrace the imperfection and mundanity of the world; accept things as they are, rather than trying to make everything over according to your ideal.

• Find friends who understand your insightful point of view and encourage you to be yourself.

• Appreciate your strengths—being insightful, idealistic, original, creative, compassionate, sincere, sensitive, loyal, organized, innovative, and determined.

INFP
Introverting   INtuiting   Feeling   Perceiving

I: is energized by their internal world.
N: focuses on visions and possibilities.
F: decides according to personal values.
P: wants things left open and flexible.

INFPs are gentle, calm, easygoing, and affirming. They puruse their inner values, are open to new ideas but can be inflexible when one of their core values feels violated. Integrity and commitment to what they believe in is essential. They have a strong inner life and complex feelings. INFPs can be hard to understand because their feelings and passionate convictions are mostly on the inside, so what is most important to them is shared with only a few.

INFPs at Work

It is hard to get your thing together if your thing is paradise on earth.
—JERRY GARCIA

- Dislike rules, orders, schedules, and deadlines.
- Have little need to impose their values on others; prefer to gently persuade, influence, and inspire.
- Are often determined achievers who go about their pursuits and tasks in a quiet, inconspicuous way.

- Can assume leadership if they are with a group whose values are in accord with their own.
- Can have trouble working in competitive environments.

- Value autonomy, dislike interruptions, and prefer doing things themselves to be sure they are done perfectly.
- Can work very patiently with complex tasks.
- Want to be appreciated and become well known for their contributions but rarely reveal this to others.
- Can be preoccupied with their own visions and expectations of themselves; measure themselves against high standards.
- Tend to see issues from all sides; can be indecisive since they have difficulty discerning what is most important to them.
- Can become disillusioned, disheartened, and discouraged if they can't find ways to realize their life goals.
- Often contain their feelings and at work can be perceived as a Thinking type.

Typical Occupations

Many different careers are suitable for INFPs. The following is a list of some occupations that have proven to be satisfying for many INFPs.

actor	musician
architect	occupational therapist
artist	photographer
composer	psychotherapist
consultant	religious educator
editor	researcher
holistic health practitioner	scientist
interpreter or translator	social scientist
journalist	speech pathologist
librarian	teacher
massage therapist	writer

INFPs in Relationships

- Value authenticity and depth in relationships.
- Are loyal, devoted, and committed to family and friends; integrity in close relationships is among their most cherished values.
- Are reticent, reserved, and relate best one-on-one or with a small group of close friends.
- Can be entertaining and whimsical when they feel comfortable.

- Have the capacity to nurture, encourage, validate, and affirm others.
- Appreciate those people who take the time to understand their dreams, goals, and aspirations.
- Are often in conflict between the need for inner solitude and a desire for connection with a few others.
- Are deeply caring but can appear indifferent and/or antisocial.
- Can either lose themselves by focusing on others or be so focused on their own dreams that they are oblivious of others' needs.
- Will often present others with their final decision rather than discussing issues as they arise.

- Can be sensitive about their environments; dislike loud noises and loud people who interrupt their inner concentration.
- Want a partner who shares their values and goals; are often disappointed if their loved one's ideals and pleasures don't match theirs.
- Are cautious about making a commitment but once made, it is usually long-lasting.

Leisure

INFPs like time alone for their many interests. They also enjoy spending time with those close to them by going to museums, films, and performances, and being in nature. They like learning and researching new things and interests. INFPs are highly reflective, especially in contemplating the mysteries and meaning of life.

Oh, for the wonder that bubbles into my soul.
—D. H. LAWRENCE

Suggestions for INFPs

- Avoid spending too much time considering possibilities and options instead of acting on them.
- Find a way to give external expression to your ideals. Share your values, visions, and emotions with those close to you.
- Take a risk by putting yourself and your work out in the world.
- Avoid focusing on other people's needs at the expense of your own. This is important in order to conserve your energy and maintain your focus.
- Learn to set boundaries, to say no, and to offer honest criticism when needed.
- Avoid procrastinating and try to stick to deadlines. Make lists of your priorities to remind you of what's most important.

WHEN DAN CAME TO THE FORK IN THE ROAD, HE TOOK IT.

- Follow through with your commitments. Beware of perfectionism which can sometimes delay you from completing tasks.
- Ask others for help instead of always relying on your own resources.
- When you have a problem, ask a friend to just listen to you and not give advice while you talk it through.
- Find people you trust to help you identify and let go of your unrealistic expectations of yourself and others.
- When conflicts arise, voice your objections; if bottled up they will explode uncontrollably later.
- Offer advice and consolation to others. You have special gifts in this area but often are reluctant to express yourself.
- Honor your values and make choices based on them even if it seems like the rest of the world does not understand them.
- Appreciate your strengths of idealism, empathy, creativity, sensitivity, self-reflection, compassion, originality, adaptability, and curiosity.

Chapter 13

Final Thoughts and Conclusions

On Relationships

As tempting as it is to believe otherwise, there really are no pat formulas for finding the right mate. Each one of us is unique and complex, and the Myers-Briggs personality descriptions do not tell us everything there is to know about ourselves or others. When we gain the knowledge of different personality types we can discover which types may be easier for us to get along with, and which ones are more challenging, thus requiring us to stretch a little more. It is not uncommon to be attracted to, and fascinated by, our opposites. There is an instinctive need to search for the undeveloped, rejected, or abandoned parts of ourselves in another person. By seeing our differences as typological rather than pathological, it can help us have a more detached perspective in the midst of conflicts. In other words, every time there is a vexing difference of opinion between two people, it doesn't mean one of them is bad or wrong.

When difficulties arise from the chafing effect of opposite styles in a relationship, it is important to remember what attracted us to the other person in the first place. In healthy relationships, there is respect and validation of the other person's qualities and an appreciation that they have strengths in certain areas, and are more comfortable in certain situations, where we are less adept.

In fact, it is possible to view these differences as a great gift. The dissimilarities found in others can enrich our lives and help us grow by exposing us to the less developed parts of our own personality. Being with our opposites can also add spice to life. To make the relationship thrive, however, it takes a lot of mutual understanding and willingness to learn the lessons offered, while appreciating the value the opposite type brings.

On the other hand, when the mate we have chosen is similar to us, we are presented with different opportunities. Being with a similar person can teach us to understand and appreciate our own most admirable qualities. It can also create its own set of problems by holding up a mirror to the traits and behaviors we don't like in ourselves. For instance, two Extraverting types can see in each other their tendency to talk too much and not spend enough time listening. Two Judging types can see how rigid they are in situations where a little flexibility would work much better. The tendencies that we are blind to in ourselves become glaringly obvious when we see someone else doing the same thing.

In addition, being with the same type of person may get boring. When people of the same preferences are together, sometimes one winds up using his or her nonpreference more, just to add variety and help the couple function better. For example, if both people are Introverting types, they may never socialize with people outside of their relationship. This may motivate one of them to use their Extraverting preference more in order to engage with the outer world.

Type doesn't explain everything and many other factors, tangible and intangible, go into good mate selection. As far as type theory goes, the best scenario in a relationship occurs when two people have some similarities to unite them so there is common ground, and some differences that complement them so there is stimulation. This kind of balance makes for a relationship that has good possibilities for pleasure, learning, and personal growth over the years.

ON PARENTING

All children are blessed with strengths and limitations. Growing up is challenging in the best of circumstances. If children learn self-acceptance at an early age, they will function better in the world and have happier lives, no matter what their type. Self-acceptance can be fostered in children by encouraging them to appreciate and enjoy their inborn preferences. When they are forced to go against their natural style, everything that they are and do seems to not be good enough. Doubt and low self-esteem are the long-lasting effects of such a parental attitude, and every aspect of adult life is impacted by it. When our natural strengths and abilities have been undermined, instead of valued for what they are, we feel like a failure because we have not lived up to unrealistic expectations. We end up believing we should be different and always have the feeling that we are falling short of the mark. The voice of the inner critic can be relentless. "You never finish things. You should be more organized." "Why can't you relate to people more easily?" "Why can't you be more practical?"

The tendency to be critical of our children's behavior often arises when we don't understand them. We may be unconsciously communicating to them how much we wish they were different. For example, an Extraverting parent may see his Introverting child's behavior as pathologically shy or withdrawn rather than recognizing that she simply has a preference for solitude and her own company. A parent with a strong Judging preference might view her Perceiving child's behavior as flaky or impractical, rather than see that she is curious and exploratory.

If we have preferences that are particularly strong, we need to be especially mindful not to force them on our children. Parents who have strong preferences and who are self-righteous can have especially damaging effects on their children. It doesn't occur to them that people should be any other way or have any other focus in life other than theirs. For example, if the parents are devoted to duty and tradition, it seems to them that everyone should honor their traditions and ways of being in the world with the same fervor. They believe their style is the only legitimate way to be. If they happen to have a child who is not wired the same way, the overwhelming tendency will be to suppress the child's natural gifts, which, of course, will not be recognized as gifts at all.

Each of us longs for love and positive regard. If we are belittled or criticized for our true Self, many will suppress what is seen as defective in order to be accepted.

By understanding that personality differences are natural, we will become more aware of our tendency to mold children into how we think they should be. It is especially important not to hold others up as role models because of a particular behavior trait, since that is one of the most effective ways to give a child the message that it is better to be something other than themselves. Statements such as, "Why can't you be more like Sarah? Look at how organized she is," are counterproductive. Far from the intended effect, they do not help our children reach the potential they can achieve, which for most parents is the ultimate goal.

On Work

The people who approach the choice of a career with confidence are often those who were encouraged early to have confidence in their inborn abilities. The reason is that faith in themselves gave them the foundation for practicing the things they were good at. It allowed them to build on their natural skills. Sometimes pursuing the work for which we are best suited, not just the job that is most available or secure, takes effort, and it requires that we take risks. We are more likely to do that if we have already had the chance to show faith and courage in the pursuit of our passions. By the time children raised this way get hired at their first job, they already know how rewarding and satisfying it can be to work at something where they can use their true strengths. For those of us who do have jobs that are interesting, but which require us to use our nondominant preferences, it is important to add balance by using our natural preferences in our leisure activities.

Regarding career choice, remember that the lists of careers for your type are only suggestions. A person can pursue any career they wish if they have the inclination or the passion.

The purpose of typology is not to label people and put them in boxes so that their possibilities become limited. Knowledge of personality types is meant to enhance and acknowledge our inherent gifts so that we can individually seek out our natural place in the scheme of things. The value of typology is not to confine, but to explain. And in the end, type and temperament are simply theories, and every human being is much more than a theory.

On Developing Our Nonpreferences

While we do change and grow and may appear to be different at various times throughout our life, our true preferences stay the same. A Thinker never becomes a

Feeler. An iNtuitive never becomes a Sensor. However, the strength of our preferences may vary considerably at different times, based on what life's situations bring out in us and what we choose to bring out in ourselves.

Learning to deliberately develop our nonpreferences, and to use whichever style is the most appropriate in a particular situation, will give us greater freedom and flexibility. The process of developing nonpreferences occurs naturally in everyone, but it can also be undertaken proactively. Midlife can bring about profound changes in people. We de-

velop new interests and activities. We open up to other points of view and new ways of doing things. As we grow and mature, we may start to pay attention to things we once overlooked or considered unimportant. In fact, this is a time when we are opening up to the hidden or less developed parts of ourselves. Within each set of preferences, the opposite of the side we usually identify with is actually very much a part of us. It is simply less available during the first half of life. Whether we develop these less visible capacities consciously or whether they develop unconsciously, as we get older their emergence adds fullness and variety to who we are. It is what Jung called the process of becoming whole.

Identifying their true personality type has been an enlightening and liberating experience for countless numbers of people who have taken the MBTI. Many people declare what a relief it is to find out that it's all right to be the kind of person they are. They can stop wishing, pointlessly, that they were like someone else.

I hope the information in this book has deepened your appreciation of yourself and that it allows you, at whatever your age, to honor and develop the natural gifts, talents, and strengths you bring to the world. For those of you who were not allowed or encouraged to be your true Self, I hope it helps you undo the critical and negative messages you may have received in childhood.

In addition, it is my wish that you can appreciate and delight in other people's styles and strengths since it will enhance the quality of your own life and relationships and make the world a more fascinating place in which to live.

I am grateful to have had the opportunity to share this valuable information, which has changed my life in such profound ways. Twenty years ago, when I read about my type, it started me on my path of self-acceptance and helped me to realize that it was all right to be me, an ENFP. I hope it has an equally powerful effect on you.

Appendix

Advanced Jungian/Myers-Briggs Type Theory

I f you want to go to a deeper level of understanding what personality type is, Jung's theory can take you beyond the individual preferences that combine to make a type. The theory provides a formula that shows you how the preferences interact and affect one another in any given combination. Jung's theory is very complex and is too involved to cover in detail in this introductory book. I will, however, briefly go over the basic elements to give you some insight into the dynamics of each type's behavior and development.

Functions and Attitudes

Here are the four pairs of preferences that have been presented in our study of the sixteen types:

1st pair	Extraverting or Introverting	E/I	Attitude
2nd pair	Sensing or iNtuiting	S/N	Function (Perception)
3rd pair	Thinking or Feeling	T/F	Function (Judgment)
4th pair	Judging or Perceiving	J/P	Attitude

Two of the pairs of preferences are mental processes, and they are called Functions.

The second pair—Sensing and iNtuiting—are Perception functions. They describe two different ways of gathering information.

The third pair—Thinking and Feeling—are Judgment functions. They describe two different ways of making decisions and coming to conclusions.

The other two pairs of preferences are called Attitudes. They describe our orientation to the world around us.

The first pair—Extraverting and Introverting—describe where we focus our energy, whether we prefer the external or internal world.

The fourth pair—Judging and Perceiving—tell how we prefer to organize the external world, using our judgment function or our perception function. This pair also points to which of the four mental functions is our dominant.

Dominant and Auxiliary Functions

Two functions show up in our four-letter type code. We will have a natural preference for one of these. This is referred to as our dominant function. It is our most developed and relied upon function and we will use it in our preferred world of extraverting or introverting. The other function that shows up in our four-letter type code acts as a support to the dominant. It is called the auxiliary function, and we will use it in our less preferred world of extraverting or introverting. This means that our auxiliary function will be used in the opposite world from our dominant.

Our dominant and auxiliary functions need to work together to provide balance for our personality. They provide us with ways to both gather information and make decisions, as well as how to deal with our inner and outer worlds.

Finding Your Dominant and Auxiliary Functions

- If the last letter of your type is J (Judging), you will use your Judgment function (Thinking or Feeling) in your external world. You will use your Perception function (Sensing or iNtuiting) in your internal world.
- If the last letter of your type is P (Perceiving), you will use your Perception function (Sensing or iNtuiting) in your external world and your Judgment function (Thinking or Feeling) in your internal world.
- If the first letter of your type is I (Introverting), the function you use in your preferred inner world is your dominant, the other function is your auxiliary.
- If the first letter of your type is E (Extraverting), the function you use in your preferred outer world is your dominant, the other function is your auxiliary.

Tertiary and Inferior Functions

Our less developed functions, the two that do not show up in our four-letter type code, have a place in our personality too. The opposite of the auxiliary function is the tertiary function. It is often not very well developed, but we do have some access to it. The opposite of the dominant function is the inferior function. It is used in the opposite attitude (Extraverting or Introverting) of our dominant. It receives the least energy and attention and is the most difficult for us to use consciously. It is the function that often appears repressed and least developed.

The Order of the Functions

The following chart lists the order of the functions for the sixteen types.

	DOMINANT		AUXILIARY		TERTIARY	INFERIOR	
ESTP	E	Sensing	I	Thinking	Feeling	I	iNtuiting
ESFP	E	Sensing	I	Feeling	Thinking	I	iNtuiting
ISTJ	I	Sensing	E	Thinking	Feeling	E	iNtuiting
ISFJ	I	Sensing	E	Feeling	Thinking	E	iNtuiting
ENTP	E	iNtuiting	I	Thinking	Feeling	I	Sensing
ENFP	E	iNtuiting	I	Feeling	Thinking	I	Sensing
INTJ	I	iNtuiting	E	Thinking	Feeling	E	Sensing
INFJ	I	iNtuiting	E	Feeling	Thinking	E	Sensing
ESTJ	E	Thinking	I	Sensing	iNtuiting	I	Feeling
ENTJ	E	Thinking	I	iNtuiting	Sensing	I	Feeling
ISTP	I	Thinking	E	Sensing	iNtuiting	E	Feeling
INTP	I	Thinking	E	iNtuiting	Sensing	E	Feeling
ESFJ	E	Feeling	I	Sensing	iNtuiting	I	Thinking
ENFJ	E	Feeling	I	iNtuiting	Sensing	I	Thinking
ISFP	I	Feeling	E	Sensing	iNtuiting	E	Thinking
INFP	I	Feeling	E	iNtuiting	Sensing	E	Thinking

NOTE: E or I in front of a function indicates whether its attitude or orientation for that type is extraverted or introverted. There is no agreement among type authors on whether the tertiary function is normally used in the same attitude as the auxiliary or the opposite. Some say it doesn't matter, as the third function has a "swing" role. That is why the tertiary column of this chart does not list an E or I prefix as the other columns do.

Type Development

Type theory can be used to explain and in some ways foster our growth and development over the course of our lifetime. According to Jung, an individual's growth process is called Individuation. This refers to the work of separating from the culture and society and making ourselves whole, using all facets of our personality, distinct from the expectations of the collective. In short, it means becoming our true Self.

According to type development theory, in the first twenty years or so of life, our energy and attention are absorbed in developing our dominant function, balanced by a healthy auxiliary function. The emergence of clear dominant and auxiliary functions gives our personality consistency, predictability, and effectiveness.

Later in life, more energy and attention are given to our less preferred functions (the tertiary and inferior). This can give our personality balance and flexibility. The ideal of type development is to have access to whichever function is most called for in a given situation.

Type development is different for different people, depending on life's circumstances. Some people are faced with challenges in life that can push them to develop their less preferred functions earlier. For other people, type development is a slow process. Some of us reach midlife and find that we have not fully developed one or both of our preferred functions. Even if we find ourselves developing late in life, growth and development are still possible.

Emergence and development of the functions and attitudes are instinctive processes over which we have limited conscious influence. Environment, parenting, and schooling affect them greatly. Not all authors or scholars agree that we can consciously affect development of our functions. However, being aware of what our less developed functions need for full expression of our personality can certainly support the individuation process.

Three sources for further reading about type development are: *Gifts Differing* by Isabel Myers and Peter Myers, *Type Dynamics and Development* by Linda Kirby and Kathy Myers, and *In the Grip of the Inferior Function* by Naomi Quenk. All three are publications of Consulting Psychologists Press.

Combining the Myers-Briggs Types with the Enneagram

There are many different systems that exist for studying the human personality. The two that I have found to be the most comprehensive and dynamic are the Myers-Briggs and the Enneagram. I have studied each one separately and discovered that combining the two can offer even greater insight than either one standing alone.

The Myers-Briggs system looks at how we come into the world, at our inborn preferences. It focuses on our strengths and on the desires that motivate our behavior. It encourages self-acceptance and tolerance.

The Enneagram looks at how we adapt to the world. It focuses on the habits of mind that limit us, and the needs that motivate our behavior. It encourages expanding our limited view of ourselves and the world and breaking through our psychological blocks.

When you understand your own or someone else's Myers-Briggs type and Enneagram type, it gives you even more insight into a person's underlying motivations. For example, two INFPs will have a lot in common, but when we add the filter of their Enneagram type, it can explain some underlying differences in their motivations. On the Enneagram, many INFPs are Fours (Romantics) and many others are Nines (Peacemakers). An INFP who is a Four is motivated by the need to understand and express her deepest feelings, to discover what is authentic in herself. An INFP who is a Nine is motivated by the need to keep the peace and create a harmonious and comfortable life. Adding this information to your understanding of what motivates an INFP offers a great deal more depth and complexity to the type.

For people studying the Enneagram, knowing about Myers-Briggs types can be helpful in the same way. A Nine who is an INFP will manifest some very different behaviors than a Nine who is an ISFJ. For example, an INFP Nine will tend to be more idealistic, individualistic, and interested in the world of ideas and possibilities. An ISFJ Nine will tend to be more traditional, realistic, and down-to-earth.

I will give you a simplified explanation of the Enneagram system, along with a brief description of the nine Enneagram types. I have also included a chart correlating the two systems. The data is based on over one thousand people. It indicates which types on the Myers-Briggs show a high percentage of being a certain type on the Enneagram, and vice versa.

If you would like to learn more and read an introductory book on the system, I suggest you read *The Enneagram Made Easy*.

The Enneagram

The Enneagram is a system of nine personality types whose roots go back many centuries. It is believed to have been taught orally in secret Sufi brotherhoods in the Middle East. The Russian mystic and spiritual teacher Gurdjieff introduced it to Europe in the 1920s. It arrived in the United States in the late 1960s through Oscar Ichazo.

The system is represented by a circle containing a nine-pointed starlike shape. *Ennea* is Greek for the number nine, and *gram* means a drawing or something written.

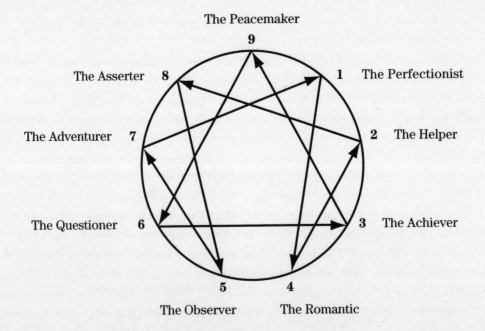

The nine personality types in the Enneagram are based on coping strategies we developed in childhood to deal with the outer world. These strategies may seem to work on one level, but they also limit our view of reality and create habitual ways in which we see and respond to life. The Enneagram looks at the needs that motivate what we do and helps us make sense of our own and others' behavior. We may all relate to some of the qualities of the various Enneagram types. However, each person has only one core type that represents their underlying motivation. Whatever type you are, you remain it for life, but you may move up and down the scale of healthy or unhealthy behavior of that particular type.

A Brief Description of the Nine Enneagram Types

ONE: *Perfectionists* are motivated by the need to live the right way. This includes improving themselves, others, and the world around them. They try to avoid criticism by doing things perfectly. Ones have a strong inner critic or conscience; they live by an internal list of rules, and discipline themselves to do what they should do. Healthy Ones are self-disciplined, hardworking, organized, conscientious, and productive. They have high standards and moral principles. Unhealthy Ones can be rigid, inflexible, controlling, self-righteous, overly serious, and hypercritical of themselves and others.

TWO: *Helpers* are motivated by the need to be loved, appreciated, and needed. They take pride in their ability to make people feel special and to anticipate and fulfill other people's needs better than anyone else. They appear cheerful, self-sufficient, and confident and are often unaware of their own needs. Healthy Twos are warm, generous, empathic, enthusiastic, and nurturing. They relate easily to people, enjoy giving to others, and are capable of unconditional love. Unhealthy Twos can be manipulative, clingy, indirect, possessive, martyrlike, and preoccupied with gaining approval.

THREE: *Achievers* are motivated by the need to be productive, efficient, admired, and successful at whatever they do. Avoiding failure is very important to them. Life is a series of tasks and goals to be completed and they keep pushing themselves to achieve more. They are often disconnected from their deeper feelings and lose an inner sense of themselves. Healthy Threes are energetic, charming, optimistic, confident, self-assured, and competent. They make good leaders who motivate others to live up to their potential. Unhealthy Threes can be vain, overly competitive, deceitful, superficial, narcissistic, opportunistic, and prone to putting on facades to impress people.

FOUR: *Romantics* are motivated by the need to understand and express their deepest feelings and to discover what is authentic in themselves. They want to feel special and unique, and avoid being seen as ordinary. Their attention is focused on whatever is missing, distant, and idealized. Healthy Fours are imaginative, sensitive, intuitive, creative, and compassionate. They are introspective, self-aware, and in touch with the hidden depths of human nature. Unhealthy Fours can be self-absorbed, hypersensitive, impractical, self-loathing, moody, depressed, and envious of those who seem more fulfilled than they are.

FIVE: *Observers* are motivated by the need to gain knowledge and to be independent and self-sufficient. They observe life from a distance, guard their privacy and space, and avoid being engulfed by others. They feel more safe and in control when thinking and analyzing than when in their feelings. They are individualistic and not influenced by social pressure or material possessions. Healthy Fives are objective, focused, calm, perceptive, insightful, and curious. They have ingenious insight. Unhealthy Fives can be intellectually arrogant, withholding, controlled, cynical, negative, standoffish, and stingy.

SIX: *Questioners* are motivated by the need to feel secure and in control, and to have safety and predictability. Feeling a sense of belonging and finding someone trustworthy to depend on is important to a Six. Sixes scan for danger and potential threat and anticipate where fear might arise. Some Sixes are phobic and withdraw to protect themselves, whereas others are counterphobic and confront fearful situations head-on, even seek them out. Healthy Sixes are trustworthy, responsible, alert, insightful, loyal, compassionate, and sympathetic to underdog causes. Unhealthy Sixes can be hypervigilant, indecisive, defensive, testy, self-defeating, paranoid, and preoccupied with worst-case scenarios.

SEVEN: *Adventurers* are motivated by the need to be happy and to stay busy by keeping their options open and constantly making plans for new experiences. They view life as a fun-filled adventure, yet they also want to contribute to the world. Boredom, suffering, painful emotions, and the everyday drudgeries of life are avoided. Sevens are constant seekers of excitement. Healthy Sevens are optimistic, enthusiastic, spontaneous, idealistic, curious, generous, and often multitalented. They uplift and enliven others and are fun to be around. Unhealthy Sevens can be self-centered, self-indulgent, insensitive, narcissistic, hyperactive, undisciplined, and have problems with completion and long-term commitments.

EIGHT: *Asserters* are motivated by the need to feel powerful and self-reliant, and to have control over their lives. They avoid being weak, vulnerable, controlled, or being taken advantage of. Being respected for their strength is more important to them than being liked. They are earthy and lusty, and they go after whatever they want. They tend to milk enjoyment out of life. They are natural leaders who want to make an impact on the world. Healthy Eights are confident, direct, decisive, courageous, and protective of their loved ones. Unhealthy Eights can be aggressive, confrontive, domineering, self-centered, insensitive, and prone to excess.

NINE: *Peacemakers* are motivated by the need to keep the peace and to create a harmonious and comfortable life. They erase their own needs and priorities to accommodate others and to avoid conflict. They are disconnected from their own emotions, especially their anger. They like to merge with others and with their environment, and they gain their sense of self through these connections. Healthy Nines are adaptable, compassionate, easygoing, supportive, patient, and nonjudgmental; they go with the flow. Unhealthy Nines can be indecisive, spaced-out, apathetic, undisciplined, unassertive, passive-aggressive, and stubborn.

Enneagram Types

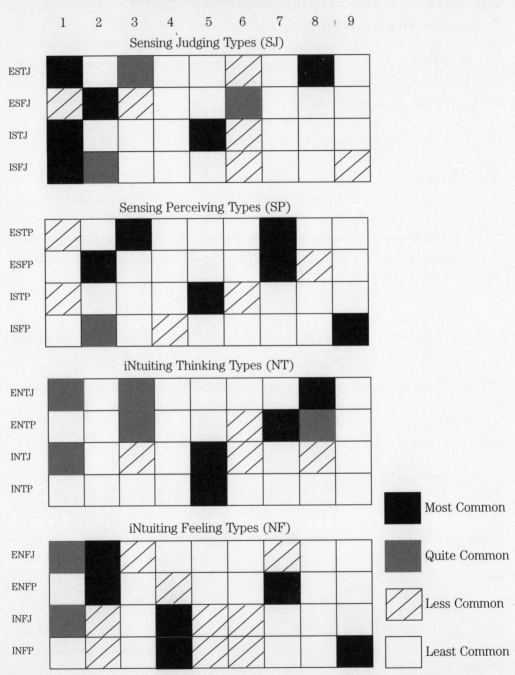

Percentage Distributions of the Types in the United States by Gender

	Males	Females			Males	Females
SJs				**NTs**		
ESTJ	12.9%	7.3%		**ENTJ**	3.5%	2.1%
ESFJ	4.7%	14.1%		**ENTP**	6.7%	2.8%
ISTJ	19.4%	12.3%		**INTJ**	4.8%	2.2%
ISFJ	6.3%	16.2%		**INTP**	6.5%	4.0%
	43.3%	49.9%			21.5%	11.1%
SPs				**NFs**		
ESTP	6.2%	3.6%		**ENFJ**	1.5%	3.4%
ESFP	4.0%	7.2%		**ENFP**	6.0%	6.6%
ISTP	8.7%	4.3%		**INFJ**	2.0%	3.1%
ISFP	2.3%	6.4%		**INFP**	4.5%	4.2%
	21.2%	21.5%			14.0%	17.3%

Reprinted and adapted from "The Distribution of MBTI Types in the United States" by Allen L. Hammer and Wayne D. Mitchell, published in the *Journal of Psychological Type*, Volume 37, 1996, pp. 2–15. Copyright © 1996 by Thomas G. Carskadon, Editor/Publisher.

Resources

Books

Brownsword, Alan. *It Takes All Types!* San Anselmo, CA: Baytree Publication Company, 1987.

Hirsh, Sandra, and Jean Kummerow. *Life Types.* New York: Warner Books, 1989.

Jung, Carl. *Psychological Types.* New York: Harcourt, Brace, 1923.

Keirsey, David, and Marilyn Bates. *Please Understand Me.* Del Mar, CA: Prometheus Nemesis Books, 1978.

Kroeger, Otto, and Janet Thuesen. *Type Talk.* New York: Delacorte Press, 1988.

———. *Type Talk at Work: How the 16 Types Determine Your Success on the Job.* New York: Delacorte Press, 1992.

Myers, Isabel Briggs, with Mary McCaulley. *Manual: A Guide to the Development and Use of the Myers-Briggs Type Indicator.* Palo Alto, CA: Consulting Psychologists Press, 1985.

———, with Peter B. Myers. *Gifts Differing.* Palo Alto, CA: Consulting Psychologists Press, 1995.

Quenk, Naomi L. *Beside Ourselves: Our Hidden Personality in Everyday Life.* Palo Alto, CA: Consulting Psychologists Press, 1993.

Tieger, Paul, and Barbara Barron-Tieger. *Do What You Are.* Boston: Little, Brown, 1992.

———. *Nurture by Nature: Understand Your Child's Personality Type—And Become a Better Parent.* Boston: Little, Brown, 1997.

Booklets

DiTibererio, John K., and Allen L. Hammer. *Introduction to Type in College.* Palo Alto, CA: Consulting Psychologists Press, 1993.

Hammer, Allen L. *Introduction to Type and Careers.* Palo Alto, CA: Consulting Psychologists Press, 1993.

Hirsh, Sandra, and Jean Kummerow. *Introduction to Type in Organizations.* Palo Alto, CA: Consulting Psychologists Press, 1990.

Isachsen, Olaf, and Linda V. Berens. *Working Together: A Personality Centered Approach to Management.* San Juan Capistrano, CA: Institute for Management Development, 1995.

Myers, Isabel Briggs. *Introduction to Type* (fifth edition). Palo Alto, CA: Consulting Psychologists Press, 1993.

Myers, Katharine D., and Linda K. Kirby. *Introduction to Type Dynamics and Development.* Palo Alto, CA: Consulting Psychologists Press, 1994.

Organizations

Association for Psychological Type (APT)
9140 Ward Parkway
Kansas City, MO 64114
Ask about local chapters in your area or country.

Center for Applications of Psychological Type (CAPT)
2720 N.W. 6th Street
Gainesville, FL 32609

Consulting Psychologists Press, Inc. (CPP)
3803 East Bayshore Road
Palo Alto, CA 94303

Otto Kroeger Associates
Fairfax Crossroads
3605-C Chain Bridge Road
Fairfax, VA 22030

The Temperament Research Institute
16152 Beach Boulevard, Suite 179
Huntington Beach, CA 92647

Type Resources, Inc.
101 Chestnut Street, H-135
Gaithersburg, MD 20877

Zeisset Associates
2443 Sewell
Lincoln, NE 68502

Enneagram Books

Baron, Renee, and Elizabeth Wagele. *The Enneagram Made Easy.* San Francisco: Harper, 1994.
———. *Are You My Type, Am I Yours?* San Francisco: Harper, 1995.

FOR THE BEST IN PAPERBACKS, LOOK FOR THE

In every corner of the world, on every subject under the sun, Penguin represents quality and variety—the very best in publishing today.

For complete information about books available from Penguin—including Penguin Classics, Penguin Compass, and Puffins—and how to order them, write to us at the appropriate address below. Please note that for copyright reasons the selection of books varies from country to country.

In the United States: Please write to *Penguin Group (USA), P.O. Box 12289 Dept. B, Newark, New Jersey 07101-5289* or call 1-800-788-6262.

In the United Kingdom: Please write to *Dept. EP, Penguin Books Ltd, Bath Road, Harmondsworth, West Drayton, Middlesex UB7 0DA.*

In Canada: Please write to *Penguin Books Canada Ltd, 10 Alcorn Avenue, Suite 300, Toronto, Ontario M4V 3B2.*

In Australia: Please write to *Penguin Books Australia Ltd, P.O. Box 257, Ringwood, Victoria 3134.*

In New Zealand: Please write to *Penguin Books (NZ) Ltd, Private Bag 102902, North Shore Mail Centre, Auckland 10.*

In India: Please write to *Penguin Books India Pvt Ltd, 11 Panchsheel Shopping Centre, Panchsheel Park, New Delhi 110 017.*

In the Netherlands: Please write to *Penguin Books Netherlands bv, Postbus 3507, NL-1001 AH Amsterdam.*

In Germany: Please write to *Penguin Books Deutschland GmbH, Metzlerstrasse 26, 60594 Frankfurt am Main.*

In Spain: Please write to *Penguin Books S. A., Bravo Murillo 19, 1° B, 28015 Madrid.*

In Italy: Please write to *Penguin Italia s.r.l., Via Benedetto Croce 2, 20094 Corsico, Milano.*

In France: Please write to *Penguin France, Le Carré Wilson, 62 rue Benjamin Baillaud, 31500 Toulouse.*

In Japan: Please write to *Penguin Books Japan Ltd, Kaneko Building, 2-3-25 Koraku, Bunkyo-Ku, Tokyo 112.*

In South Africa: Please write to *Penguin Books South Africa (Pty) Ltd, Private Bag X14, Parkview, 2122 Johannesburg.*